P9-CDW-747

HANSONS
HALF-MARATHON
METHOD

HANSONS
HALF-MARATHON
METHOD

Run Your Best Half-Marathon the Hansons Way

LUKE HUMPHREY
WITH KEITH & KEVIN HANSON

Boulder, Colorado

Copyright © 2014 by Luke Humphrey

All rights reserved. Printed in the United States of America.

No part of this book may be reproduced, stored in a retrieval system, or transmitted, in any form or by any means, electronic or photocopy or otherwise, without the prior written permission of the publisher, except in the case of brief quotations within critical articles and reviews.

▼velopress®

3002 Sterling Circle, Suite 100
Boulder, Colorado 80301-2338 USA
(303) 440-0601 · Fax (303) 444-6788 · E-mail velopress@competitorgroup.com

Distributed in the United States and Canada by Ingram Publisher Services

Library of Congress Cataloging-in-Publication Data
Humphrey, Luke, 1981–
   Hansons half-marathon method : run your best half-marathon the Hansons way /
Luke Humphrey, with Keith and Kevin Hanson.
      pages cm
   Includes index.
   ISBN 978-1-937715-19-9 (pbk. : alk. paper)
1. Long-distance running—Training. I. Hanson, Keith. II. Hanson, Kevin. III. Title.
   GV1065.H77 2014
   796.42'5—dc23
                         2013050470

For information on purchasing VeloPress books, please call (800) 811-4210, ext. 2138, or visit www.velopress.com.

Cover design by Ozzie Thoreson
Interior design by Vicki Hopewell
Composition by Jessica Xavier
Illustrations by Visual Health Information and Nicole Kaufman
Tables 8.1 and A.2 adapted with permission from Monique Ryan, *Sports Nutrition for Endurance Athletes*, 3rd ed. (Boulder, CO: VeloPress, 2012).

Text set in Archer

14   15   16   /   10   9   8   7   6   5   4   3   2

Contents

Foreword

Congratulations! In your hands you have the ultimate guide to adventure. Sure, it's also a guide to your best half-marathon yet, and the following pages will give you the training plans, graphs, numbers, and science you need to get to your goals. But it is so much more than that. While I can't be sure that you'll run your fastest—that part is up to you—I can tell you that your adventure begins as soon as you lace up your running shoes. In this book you are the captain of your own adventure; you decide where, when, and how far you wish to go.

In your hands you also have the ultimate self-help book. Thumb through the pages and you may not see exercises on self-esteem building or the keys to happiness. But I dare you to head out the door, log some miles, and not feel like you made you a better you. Just try and go for a run and not let your mind wander to those places that haven't gotten the proper attention. You'll likely find that every mile and every workout is a perfect opportunity to spend some time on yourself, and I suspect you will learn a lot about you in the process.

I've been fortunate enough to get to run all over the United States, as well as in Japan, Europe, and the Middle East; it's been an amazing adventure. But the truth is that some of the best runs I have taken involved getting lost just a few miles from home and stumbling upon that hidden coffee shop—the one I'd never see from the main road—or getting lost in a conversation during a run and forgetting it's 34 degrees and raining. I've run races that people said "awed" them, and yet I've discovered the most gratifying running moments when nobody was watching. Yes, I'd be the first to admit that there's something incredibly painful about heading out for a 5:00 a.m. run, but when you crest that final hill and see an amazing sunrise, it is all worthwhile. You earned a sunrise that the sleepy world is missing out on. And there is something therapeutic about losing track of your pace while sorting through a day's problems. Or, better yet, forgetting your problems by getting caught up in your pace.

So, yes, congratulations! You've stumbled upon the ultimate adventure and maybe the key to happiness; all it requires is for you to get out the front door and make it happen. I wish you the best of luck meeting all of your running goals and running your fastest half-marathon ever. I can't promise you will hit every goal, but I can promise you this: the journey along the way will be worth it.

So as you chase your goals, remember to enjoy the journey because the *process* of becoming a faster you is often far more satisfying than just *being* a faster you.

—DESIREE LINDEN
2012 U.S. Olympic marathoner

Acknowledgments

I owe the world to Kevin and Keith Hanson for giving me the reins on this project and letting me make it my own. I have learned much of what I know from their talent, dedication, and coaching. To talk with them not only about the "what" and "how" of their programs but also the "why" is like being able to open an encyclopedia and find the answer to almost any training question imaginable.

I must also thank Casey Blaine at VeloPress for her passion for this project—and for never getting too mad at me for missing a deadline. She enthusiastically tweaked the manuscript into a comprehensible form, making sure that the idea I was trying to convey was never lost.

Since the release of our first book, *Hansons Marathon Method*, my coaching business has expanded beyond my wildest dreams. In fact, it grew so quickly, I was blindsided a bit and we had to scramble to ensure our quality wasn't lost in the growth. For that, I thank Corey Kubatzky, my director of operations, who ended up doing a lot of small, thankless projects so I could continue to coach, write, and keep my sanity.

Last but not least, I am so grateful to my wife for supporting me through this task of writing a book. There were lots of late nights reading and writing material for this book. My daughter, Josephine, also deserves some credit for helping daddy type, because, well, she likes technology. Big thanks to my girls.

Introduction

In 1999, brothers Kevin and Keith Hanson were successful coaches and running-store owners in the Detroit metropolitan area. But they had a vision—to change the course of American distance running—and with the help of Brooks Sports started the Hansons-Brooks Distance Project, an Olympic training program for postcollegiate athletes. Fifteen years later, the program has a voice and presence at the most elite level of the sport, producing Olympians and World Championship qualifiers at the half- and full marathon distances.

Over the years, the brothers showed that they can train world-class runners, but around Michigan, they have always been best known for helping everyday runners to achieve their best performances. That's where I (Luke) fit in. In 2004, I joined the program as a fairly decent young runner but have since matured into a two-time Olympic Trials qualifier and sub-1:04:00 half-marathoner with Kevin and Keith as my mentors. Aside from being able to run pretty far at a solid pace, I also have a master's degree in exercise science and began teaching the Hansons Method to our running groups in 2006. As the elite program gained success, this renegade training approach began attracting more and more attention. People started asking questions, wanting to know more, and magazine articles, although they were terrific for exposure, couldn't provide the full picture. In 2012, we were given an avenue to provide the world with the comprehensive knowledge of the Hansons Method for the marathon.

When our first book, *Hansons Marathon Method*, was released, the response was wonderful; almost immediately, however, people were asking, "How do I adapt this for a half-marathon?" This perhaps is not a surprising question if you look at the numbers. According to Running USA, each year, the half-marathon has hundreds of thousands more participants than the marathon. In 2012, the number of half-marathon finishers totaled about 1.85 million, compared with about 487,000 in the marathon. And that number is only growing.

The bottom line is that there are a lot more people lacing up for a 13.1-mile race. Most half-marathoners fall into one of these four general categories:

VETERAN RUNNERS // These runners have logged plenty of miles over the years and have probably run several half-marathons in the past. They are looking to take their previous half-marathon performances to the next level. They have probably run at least one marathon in the past, as well. This is a pretty competitive group.

RECREATIONAL RUNNERS // While members of this group are new to the half-marathon distance, they are not running newbies, having completed a number of shorter races. This group is looking to establish a half-marathon baseline, usually with plans to run another half-marathon in the future and probably to move up to the next level after running the *half-marathon*.

NOVICE RUNNERS // The novice group includes newer runners looking to knock "13.1" off their bucket list, as well as those running for charity groups. Many of these runners will leave half-marathoning behind once they finish the race. The novice group is prevalent in the half-marathon world, due in part to the robust charity scene. I have many clients who run a race for a loved one while representing that person's cause, and it is often more realistic for them to commit to a half-marathon distance than to the full marathon.

BEGINNING RUNNERS // This group includes a large contingent of charity runners, as well as people who decide to do a race as a way to begin a fitness program. While I certainly would not advise complete beginners to take on a full marathon as their first race, the half-marathon distance is much more readily achievable, with less potential for injury. Out of this group, some will continue to run, moving into another group, and some will abandon the sport following their race.

When we discussed training for a full marathon, we talked about newbies being convinced that they can have it all and not sacrifice any of their free time—or their toenails! For many, that time commitment is probably a pretty big turnoff for the marathon, especially when you are training through summer barbecues and days on the beach, but we never wanted to make you feel that you were about to embark on a walk in the park. Well, when we cut the distance in half, the training doesn't have to be such a commitment, and that probably holds a strong appeal for about 1.8 million people in the United States.

With all of this said, make no bones about it: The Hansons Method is still focused on helping you run the best you can. So, while you may not be cursing us during the middle of a tempo run, you may still grumble under your breath.

A training plan with minimal mileage and three running days per week can be a great way to ease into the sport and build a foundation without getting injured; once the decision is made to make the leap to the marathon, however, it simply isn't enough. For the half-marathon, it may be less detrimental, but it still may not provide you with everything you need to be prepared for the race. Although these plans usually assist runners in reaching their main goal, which is to finish, the by-product is often a dislike of the sport. Because the greatest predictor of adherence to any type of exercise is enjoyment, this certainly isn't a recipe for long-term success in running.

By charting a course for a successful and enjoyable half-marathon experience, the Hansons Method seeks to encourage the crossing of multiple finish lines of multiple race distances. Training should always allow you to transition to different race distances without a major change in overall training philosophy. Unlike a number of the other popular training plans out there, our approach will transform you into not only a finisher but a longtime competitor. We take a straight-talk approach when it comes to teaching you about half-marathon training; we won't sugarcoat, offer any supposed shortcuts, or treat you with condescension. Indeed, running itself wouldn't be a big deal if it didn't require a little blood, a lot of sweat, and perhaps a few tears.

PART I

the
approach

Hansons training philosophy

THIS CHAPTER TAKES A close look at the philosophies that lay the groundwork for the Hansons Half-Marathon Method. You may think that understanding our philosophy is optional, but I strongly encourage you to take time to read this section. Studies show that we are far more likely to adopt and embrace new habits and behaviors if we understand why we are doing something.

The building blocks of this program rest on the teachings of famed coach Arthur Lydiard. Widely credited with popularizing the sport of running, Lydiard led a long line of runners to realize their Olympic dreams. As a result, his ideas about training had a major influence on the development of our methods. As taught by Lydiard, the idea of cumulative fatigue serves as an underlying foundation of all of our training plans.

Cumulative fatigue comes from a slow buildup (but not to the point of overtraining) of fatigue via the days, weeks, and months of consistent training. In other words, cumulative fatigue results

> **cumulative fatigue** is the accumulation of fatigue over days, weeks, and even months of consistent training.

from repetitive training that doesn't allow for full recovery between training days. It emphasizes a concerted, strategic approach to half-marathon training rather than a number of disparate training days strung together at random. The fundamental principle of cumulative fatigue runs throughout the Hansons Half-Marathon Method and consists of five components:

// mileage
// intensity
// balance
// consistency
// active recovery

If you omit one component of the cumulative fatigue philosophy, you interfere with the others, creating a domino effect that limits the physiological adaptations necessary for successful half-marathoning.

Mileage: Strategic weekly volume

The biggest problem with many half-marathon training plans is that they are tailored to fit what the average runner wants, not what he or she needs. These programs usually place a majority of the weekly mileage on Saturday and Sunday, when runners have the most time available. Roughly the same amount of mileage is then spread over a few days of the workweek. This can mean that all the prescribed weekday runs are higher-intensity workouts, leaving few opportunities for easy runs and the accumulation of important training mileage. Since the weekday runs in those plans are mostly high-intensity, it takes a runner longer to recover, causing the easier runs to fall by the wayside. Even if these plans did specify running on the interim days, runners would likely be too tired from the previous workouts.

Adequate weekly mileage plays an important role in the cumulative fatigue process. Increasing mileage comes along with increasing training from 3–4 days a week to 6 days a week. This doesn't necessarily mean adding intensity but rather more easy mileage. The Hansons Half-Marathon Method shows you how to add that mileage while controlling your pace to avoid overworking yourself. Consider the fact that runners training for a 5K will put in four to six times their actual race distance in mileage each week (see Table 1.1). Although the average half-marathoner won't put in four to five times the half-marathon distance on a weekly basis (50–65 miles), it is reasonable to run roughly three times the distance per week (35–45 miles).

TABLE **1.1**	WEEKLY MILEAGE BASED ON LEVEL AND EVENT		
	BEGINNER	COMPETITIVE	ELITE
5K (3.1 mi.)	15–25	40–50	90+
10K (6.2 mi.)	25–30	45–55	90+
half-marathon (13.1 mi.)	30–40	50–60	100+
marathon (26.2 mi.)	40–50	60–70	110+

Although runners preparing for the half-marathon realize that they will need to run more mileage than they would need to for the 5K, it can be a bit intimidating to look at some of these totals. Runners, especially newer ones, will look a few months ahead and doubt that they will be able to handle the training. What those runners lack is confidence. We tell runners to start at the ridiculous, or what they think is completely beyond their capabilities, and work backward until they reach a point that is both mentally and physically manageable. While 35–45 miles per week may sound ridiculous on day one, focusing on what you have to do in the present is key. You will be surprised by what you are able to handle a few months down the line.

Again and again we have seen that athletes who give their bodies adequate time to adapt to new training stresses are able to tolerate much more than they ever imagined to be feasible. Our program works to take you up the mileage ladder one rung at a time, starting with lower mileage and gradually increasing both mileage and intensity. As I like to say to our athletes, "If you want to build a house, you must first create a structure to hold it up." The volume of mileage builds a foundation that allows all the other variables to work.

Intensity: Physiological adaptations

In addition to an appropriate amount of total weekly mileage, our plans stand apart from the rest in terms of pace and intensity. These factors are inextricably linked because if workouts are overly difficult, you're going to be too tired to reach your weekly mileage quotas. In the Hansons-Brooks Distance Project, the competition can be fierce among our elite athletes. Teaching proper pacing is perhaps our biggest struggle with runners. During workouts, Kevin and Keith always seem to know when an athlete has developed an "I know you're fast, but I'm just a little bit faster" mentality toward another runner. As a means of emphasizing the importance of pace and punishing runners who run faster than they are instructed to, they dole out push-ups for every second someone is too fast. After a few penalty push-ups, the athlete inevitably pulls back on the reins and falls into step.

While we won't make you do push-ups when you falter in your pacing, pacing does remain an important component of cumulative fatigue. The majority of our suggested mileage is run at anaerobic threshold (lactate threshold) pace or slower. You may wonder, "How am I supposed to get faster if I'm running slower?" In the next chapter, we will explain the many beneficial adaptations that come with endurance training, such as mitochondria development, muscle fiber adaptations, and the ability to burn fat as fuel. Exercise physiologists have discovered that these adaptations are best elicited through a pace that is slower than anaerobic threshold pace. This improves your running by pushing the aerobic threshold, anaerobic threshold, and aerobic capacity up from the bottom instead of trying to pull them up from the top. Whether it is an easy running day or a hard workout, executing the task at the appropriate pace is integral to the entire training system.

Easy runs are often misunderstood as junk mileage or filler training. The truth is, easy runs make up a big percentage of the training week, and when they are run at the optimal intensities, they promote a wide array of favorable physiological adaptations. Despite this fact, both novices and experienced runners struggle with properly pacing these relaxed workouts. Newer runners tend to run their easy days too hard because the gradual training plan feels too easy. Most of the time, the intensity evens out as mileage increases and the runner is too tired to maintain that pace throughout the week. However, as a coach, I would prefer to have you adjust the pace to your half-marathon goal and train properly from day one. This allows you to increase your mileage and intensity safely over weeks and months. More experienced runners tend to get overzealous in their training, believing that faster is better, especially for those moving up from running competitively at shorter distances. Runners in this situation will quickly be benched as a result of overtraining if they don't temper their excitement and allow easy runs to truly be easy. Regardless of your current level, when we instruct you to run "easy," we really mean easy. Once you add in hard workouts, these easy days will serve as active recovery to allow your body to bounce back and prepare for the next workout.

Proper pacing during hard workouts is equally vital. We cannot stress enough that workouts are designed to spur specific physiological adaptations; they are not to be run as hard as you can to see who is the last person standing. For instance, tempo runs and strength workouts develop the anaerobic threshold, but that doesn't mean you should be running a tempo workout faster than anaerobic threshold pace. Similarly, speed workouts develop aerobic capacity and should be run just under your maximal aerobic capacity, not beyond it. Imagine if you are instructed to run 6 × 800-meter repeats at 5K pace. Let's say this pace is 6:00 minutes per mile, or 3:00 for 800 meters. If you do the first three intervals at 2:45, 2:45, and 2:55, there's a good chance the last three will be around 3:10, 3:15, and perhaps 3:10. While you averaged 3:00, you failed to hit a single interval at the prescribed pace. This means that you didn't accumulate any training at the desired pace, which was specifically set to stimulate aerobic capacity. The first three were too fast, which exceeded VO_2max, producing anaerobic energy and lactic acid. The last three were then progressively slower due to fatigue and lactic acid buildup. In the end, you drove yourself into the ground without gaining any major physiological benefits.

Now you understand why Kevin and Keith assign push-ups. By keeping your paces in check across the training spectrum, you'll tolerate higher training volumes. You'll also be more consistent in training because you won't be so worn-out that you need to take unscheduled days off or modify workouts. Cumulative fatigue is designed to make you tired, but running paces faster than prescribed will put you beyond the point of being able to recover sufficiently. That really is junk mileage.

Balance: Training equilibrium

Whether you are training for a 5K or a marathon, there should always be one constant: balance. So many programs emphasize one area of training and sacrifice others. For instance, a 5K program may focus on doing repeats on the track two times a week at the expense of a weekly long run. On the other hand, a marathon program may put sole focus on surviving weekly long runs, but no speed work is to be seen. To fully reach your potential as a runner, all the physiological systems must be incorporated into training. Remember, nothing is make-or-break. The long run won't make your half-marathon if it's the only thing you focus on. Being strong and fast and having endurance will make your half-marathon! This is why all of our programs emphasize a balanced approach to training.

The Hansons Half-Marathon Method presents you with two types of runs: easy and something of substance (SOS). SOS runs include speed workouts, strength workouts, tempo runs, and long runs. Think of these runs as workouts that require more effort than do easy days. By varying the training, you reap the necessary physiological benefits in addition to maintaining motivation. If variety is the spice of life, you'd better include a good amount of it in your training. In the same way that your mind gets bored with repetition, so does your body. When you cycle your workouts and stress each individual system, you stimulate a steady rate of physiological adaptation. By giving time and energy not just to the long run but also to easy, strength, speed, tempo, and recovery days, you'll be a stronger, more balanced runner.

There is such a thing as too much of a good thing. When you balance your training, you'll be sure to get just the right amount of each of those things.

Consistency: Sticking to the game plan

As a coach, I find that many runners struggle with training consistency. One week they run three days, the next four days, and the next week maybe only two days. This is unsurprising because each week brings its own challenges and surprises: Your boss imposes a last-minute deadline, your car breaks down, or your child gets sick. The unpredictability of life can make sticking to a training plan difficult. While training adjustments are necessary at times, a regular running schedule remains important.

Physiologically speaking, inconsistency in training makes for a never-ending struggle to maintain even a baseline of fitness. While adaptations can occur rapidly with proper training, they can also be lost with just a couple of weeks of inconsistent running. For instance, if you train 5 days a week for 3 weeks, a noticeable improvement in fitness will take place; if, however, those weeks are followed by 2 weeks of training only 2 or 3 days a week, your fitness gains will begin to retreat. It then requires 2 more weeks of consistent running to get back to the previous level. In the end, 6–8 weeks of running went by just to get you back to where you were at the third week. If life intervenes, modify training, but don't skip it. Something is always better than nothing.

To achieve this consistency, you must establish attainable goals and plan ahead. If you set your sights too high, you're likely to get discouraged when you discover you have too much on your plate. Conversely, if you set them too low, you get bored. Properly placed goals will keep you motivated to get out the door each day, even when running feels like the last thing you want to do. Planning your weekly running schedule in advance also aids in commitment. Rather than looking at the training program the morning of a workout, you know what to expect for the next 5–7 days. By penciling your runs into your day planner or posting them on your refrigerator, you can plan for hurdles that may be thrown in front of you throughout the week. If you have an early morning meeting on Tuesday, plan on running after work. If your kids have a soccer tournament all weekend, find an opening between games to fit your run in. When you schedule your runs, you are far more likely to stick to the plan and remain consistent in your training.

Active recovery: Partial rest

When it comes to cumulative fatigue, you walk a fine line between training enough and overtraining. The goal of the Hansons Method is to take you close to the line but not over it. The training you do throughout the course of the program is tough, but it will lead to a better, more enjoyable race-day result. Incomplete recovery is an important part of the training because it allows you to perform well, even when you aren't feeling 100 percent.

Whether you are doing a speed, strength, tempo, or long run, there is a general preoccupation with the idea of being "fresh" for workouts. That freshness, however, requires days off before and after workouts, which takes away from the crucial aerobic adaptations that easy runs offer. While we don't put hard workouts back-to-back, we do employ the idea of active recovery. This means that workouts are often followed by easy running days. This allows you to recover for the next hard workout without taking the day off from running. Think about it this way: After a hard workout, your muscles are depleted of glycogen and feel supremely fatigued. At this time it is important to replace that glycogen, hydrate, and allow the muscles to heal. This, however, doesn't mean you should lie inert on the couch for the next 24 hours. For one thing, you can't gain any aerobic fitness if you take the next day off. Also, you never teach your body how to deal with long-term discomfort if you always allow it to completely recover. Easy running is done at low enough intensities that you are primarily burning fat, allowing your body time to rebuild the lost carbohydrate (glycogen) stores. In addition, your muscles learn to more efficiently burn fat because they are running at a pace that promotes fat burning rather than carbohydrate depletion. The muscles also adapt to the training loads placed on them and will eventually become stronger. This means you can handle increased workloads, recover, and gain aerobic fitness faster if you just run easy on days you don't have a hard workout.

active recovery is a light workout where the heart rate is elevated but for a short period of time, such as 15–30 minutes.

While recovery is important, cumulative fatigue calls for only partial recuperation. Even after an easy-run day, your muscles may still be somewhat fatigued and glycogen stores only moderately refueled, causing you to feel slightly sluggish. This is normal. You are training your body to withstand many miles of running. Just as you may feel sluggish toward the end of the half-marathon and will need to push through, it is important to learn to keep moving forward during your training. This makes cumulative fatigue an integral part of your long runs. Although you'll have the last few days of training still in your legs, you'll be recovered enough to run the long run as desired. Our method teaches your legs to withstand the latter portion of the half-marathon by loading them with a little fatigue prior to the long runs.

Put simply, we're looking to simulate running tired. By feeling fatigued going into a workout, you know how the late stages of a race will feel. Knowing you can nail a workout while tired from regular training will boost your confidence late in the race when things get hard physically and mentally. That being said, the stress is not so great that you will need the following week to recover. Instead, the next day will be easy, and then a workout will follow a couple of days after that. Through a number of physiological adaptations, cumulative fatigue trains your body to be fully prepared for the physiological stress imparted by the half-marathon distance. As you look at our training programs, you'll notice that every 4 weeks, the mileage increases slightly via easy days, tempo runs, and long runs. As your body adapts, you vary the stress and continue the progression upward. Leading up to the big day, you will finally allow your body to fully recover, giving you that fresh feeling as you toe the line. In other words, you are ready for peak performance. Our programs are designed this way to help you feel your best during the race, not during training. After all, you never want to execute your best performance in practice.

Training for a half-marathon isn't easy, and it shouldn't be taken lightly; a few curse words may be uttered, favorite television shows missed, and social outings forgone, but you will regret nothing when you successfully cross that finish line. This entire program has been developed by great coaches who have learned from other great coaches. It is a philosophy that can transform you from a person who wants to run a half-marathon into a bona fide half-marathoner. We're here to get you there.

Understanding certain physiological principles will help you make sense of the structure of the training program. That foundation will provide the "why" while the program will provide the "what to do" and "when to do it." The structure of the Hansons Half-Marathon Method is dependent on the physiological basis of endurance running performance. By understanding these key principles, runners are less likely to make critical mistakes in their training.

The end result of all these components is the idea of cumulative fatigue. After reading the previous pages, you have, I hope, picked up on one thing—these components are all related. If you remove one or change one drastically, the whole flow of the philosophy is disrupted. The marathon training version of our program asks for a very substantial commitment. However, the beauty of the half-marathon is that the training doesn't need to consume as much of your time, and our half-marathon plan may seem like less of a risk than the marathon plan if it is very different from other types of training you have tried. It's also great for me as a coach because I can introduce you to a slimmer version of the training and then trick you into training for the full marathon later on! On a serious note, though, don't be fooled. Training for a half-marathon takes focus and a strong commitment; the results, however, will be well worth that commitment.

2

Marathon physiology

IF YOU HAVE EVER watched a track meet on TV and seen an 800-meter race (a half mile, run in two laps), you may have heard a commentator comment on how tough that race is to train for. Runners ask themselves, do I train like a 400-meter sprinter, or do I train like a miler? It's an odd distance physiologically and can be tough to dial in. The half-marathon offers a similar complication: Do I train like a 10K runner or like a marathon runner? It's a tricky question, and not all coaches agree on the answer. But, as with most problems in running, it comes down to you individually, and in this case your physiology will point you in the right direction.

I have coached a few people who excelled at shorter distance (5K and 10K) but decided they wanted to try the half-marathon distance. Unfortunately, their approach to the half-marathon, which is twice as long as a 10K, was exactly the same. Most of them were too fast in their workouts, with many of them simply trying to run hard and see how well they could hang on.

Think about it this way: Consider what goes on when you train for a 5K. First, it's a relatively short race, measured in minutes and not hours. Second, it's almost a pure speed race, meaning that we have the endurance to cover the distance, and we tend to want to see how fast we can cover it. Finally, if you go out too fast, it hurts, but the amount of suffering is limited by the amount of race left. If you do crash and burn, most likely it will be for less than a mile.

Now, extrapolate to a 13.1-mile race. If you go out too hard at this distance, you can suffer for a very long time. What this all means is that having an idea of why we are suffering and the physiological basis behind it is critical to our success. Without a basic understanding, we are liable to make the same training mistakes over and over.

Knowing about physiology, in particular for the half-marathon distance, is critical for reaching your desired race goals. For a full marathon, no matter if you are a local legend or are running your first marathon in 4-plus hours, everybody is training the same energy systems. In other words, how your body uses energy, what systems it stresses for speed and endurance, and how fast it is using those energy sources are the same for all marathoners. Success at any level in marathoning depends on how well you can adapt to specific training principles. With the half-marathon, in contrast, smart training—specifically what systems you train—is far more dependent on what kind of runner you are and your individual race goals. Generally speaking, for faster runners—those looking to run the half in under 1 hour and 45 minutes—the training emphasis should be on increasing individual lactate threshold (or anaerobic threshold). Why? Because those runners will hover around that threshold for the entire race. For runners on the other end of the spectrum (wanting to complete the half-marathon in 3-plus hours), the goal should be improving aerobic pathways, since these runners may not approach their anaerobic thresholds (at least for the same duration that the faster folks will). Runners in between the two ends of the spectrum will need a blend of everything in fairly equal proportions. A lot to take in? Don't worry, this chapter will walk you through it.

The human body is a beautifully complicated piece of machinery, but at the end of the day, if you want to race at your best, there are just five components of your physiology that you should understand. You may have heard these terms tossed about and wondered what they meant. I'll break them down to arm you with what you really need to know in your training. These five key components are as follows:

// running-specific muscles   // aerobic threshold
// VO_2 max   // running economy
// anaerobic threshold

Running muscles: Forceful influence

When it comes to physiological movers and shakers, the musculature system is king. More than 600 muscles in your body work to create motion and force. They allow your heart to beat, your eyes to move, your food to digest, and your legs to run. The three main types of muscle fibers are cardiac, smooth, and skeletal. While the cardiac muscle makes your heart beat, and the smooth muscle lines your intestines, pushing food through your system, the skeletal muscle plays the starring role in human locomotion. Skeletal muscles make running possible.

The skeletal muscles are responsible for generating physiological movement and also are where the majority of energy is stored. These muscles include slow-twitch fibers and fast-twitch fibers, the latter of which have several subcategories. Each muscle contains both types of muscle fiber, which are bound together like bundles of cable, each bundle consisting of a single type. Thousands of these bundles constitute a muscle, and each individual bundle is controlled by a single motor neuron. The motor neurons are located in the central nervous system, where they work to control muscles and, in turn, movement.

Together, the fibers and the motor neurons make up the motor unit. Because each bundle contains only one type of fiber, a bundle of slow-twitch fibers and a bundle of fast-twitch fibers will receive information from the brain via separate motor units. If one motor neuron is activated, a weak muscle contraction occurs. If multiple motor neurons are activated, a more powerful muscular contraction is created. Why is all this important? Ultimately, the structure of the skeletal muscle system dictates running ability. So the better you understand your own physiology, the smarter your training will be. Let's look closer at the types of muscle fibers.

TYPE I FIBERS (SLOW-TWITCH FIBERS)

Your family tree plays an important role in determining your potential as a runner. If your parents endowed you with an abundance of Type I muscle fibers, also called slow-twitch fibers, you have a leg up on the competition. These fibers are particularly important for endurance events because of their efficient use of fuel and their resistance to fatigue. Slow-twitch fibers are aerobic, meaning they use oxygen to transfer energy. This is a result of the fact that they have a large area of capillaries and, therefore, a much greater available supply of oxygen than do fast-twitch fibers. Additionally, these fibers have the machinery necessary for aerobic metabolism to take place. Known as the mitochondria, this machinery is often referred to as the "powerhouse of the cell." Thanks to the mitochondria, you are able to use fats and carbohydrates as fuel sources to keep your muscles working and your body running.

True to their name, the slow-twitch fibers also have a slower shortening speed than the other types of fibers, which serves an important function for endurance runners. While these fibers cannot generate as much force as the others, they supply energy at a steady rate and can generate a good amount of power for an extended period. In addition to being slower to contract, Type I fibers are only about half the diameter of fast-twitch fibers. Although they are smaller and slower, they are also more efficient and persistent, warding off fatigue during a long haul on the roads.

TYPE II FIBERS (FAST-TWITCH FIBERS)

Type II fibers, also known as fast-twitch fibers, are also genetically determined and are the slow-twitch fibers' more ostentatious counterpart. They are bigger and faster, and they pack a powerful punch, but they also fatigue rapidly. Because these fibers have very few mitochondria, they transfer energy anaerobically (without the use of oxygen). These forceful contractions use such large amounts of adenosine triphosphate (ATP), basically a high-energy molecule, that they quickly tire and become weak. That is precisely why the Olympic 100-meter champion can run a record-setting pace only for the length of the homestretch, but the marathon champion can maintain a record-setting pace for 26.2 miles. Two different muscle fiber types, two different results.

The Type II fibers are further divided into subgroups, two of the most common being Type IIa and Type IIb, also known as the intermediate fibers. The Type IIa fibers share several characteristics with slow-twitch fibers because they have more mitochondria and capillaries than other types of fast-twitch fibers. As a result, Type IIa fibers are considered to be aerobic, although they still provide a more forceful contraction than slow-twitch fibers. By contrast, Type IIb fibers contract powerfully, transfer energy anaerobically, and fatigue quickly. See Table 2.1 for a brief comparison among fiber types.

TABLE
2.1 **COMPARISON OF MUSCLE FIBER TYPES**

	TYPE I	TYPE IIA	TYPE IIB
contraction time	slow	fast	fastest
fatigue resistance	high	medium	low
force production	low	high	highest
mitochondria density	high	high	low
capillary density	high	medium	low
oxidative capacity	high	high	low

A WORKING SYSTEM

All humans have both Type I and Type II muscle fibers, but the distribution varies greatly. Most people, regardless of gender, have a Type I fiber distribution of 45–55 percent in their arms and legs. Individuals who are fitness conscious but not completely devoted to training can see a Type I distribution of around 60 percent. Meanwhile, trained distance runners tend to have a Type I distribution of 70 percent, and elite marathoners have an even greater percentage than that. Herein lies the challenge. When it comes to running a half-marathon, Runner A, who has a high proportion of Type I fibers, will naturally be better off than Runner B, who has a low Type I and low Type IIa distribution. So how does Runner B get around his own physiology?

Luckily for both runners, the body is an amazing machine that can adapt to a myriad of stresses. In the field of exercise physiology, stress denotes the repeated and intense training that leads to certain physiological adaptations. Researchers have long sought the key to muscle fiber conversion, hoping to discover how a person, such as Runner

B, could actually change the composition of her muscles via training stress. Although much of the research remains inconclusive, it is agreed that elite distance runners have a greater proportion of Type I fibers than the average recreational runner, and that those Type I fibers are necessary for a fast marathon or half-marathon performance (see Table 2.2 for a comparison among different types of runners). What we don't know is if you are genetically bound to a particular muscle fiber arrangement or if you can change it with physical training through certain training stresses. Although it may be too early to make any definite statements about conversions from Type I to Type II fibers, it has been shown that transformations can take place within the Type II fibers. Even after a relatively short training block of 10–12 weeks, a runner can display a transition from anaerobic, fatigable Type IIb fibers to the more aerobic, fatigue-resistant Type IIa fibers. This is great for an endurance runner. It shows that training elicits tangible physiological changes that create performance advantages and real improvements. There is much hope for Runner B.

TABLE 2.2 COMPARISON OF TYPE I AND II FIBERS AMONG DIFFERENT POPULATIONS			
	TYPE I	TYPE IIA	TYPE IIB
sprinter	20%	45%	35%
sedentary	40%	30%	30%
average active	50%	40%	10%
middle-distance runner	60%	35%	5%
world-class marathoner	80%	20%	<1%

MAXIMIZING MUSCLE FIBERS

Whereas all endurance athletes will benefit from fat-burning increases, glycogen saving, and having an abundance of slow-twitch fibers, there is no "one size fits all" type of muscle fiber disbursement that is best for all half-marathoners. For them, the ideal ratio depends on how fast or slow they run. For instance, faster runners may have a large number of slow-twitch fibers, but because of the intensity with which they are running, they are also probably helped a fair amount by their collection of intermediate fibers. These runners must generate a high amount of force to maintain a fast pace. Alternately, slower runners do best if they train like marathon runners, which means having mostly slow-twitch fibers and a high level of fat utilization and glycogen storage, because their intensity is lower and their time on their feet is significantly longer—perhaps double that of their faster counterparts.

Regardless of genetics, training remains a vital predictor of running performance. Although genetics dictate what kind of work you may be innately suited for, the right training helps you maximize your individual potential. We will show you how this can be done, no matter what your DNA might say. To get your muscles to respond the way you want them to on race day, you must train them to fire in a particular manner. It all starts with a signal sent from the motor units in the central nervous system, which begins by recruiting the slow-twitch fibers. You continue to rely heavily on those fibers unless you do one of the following:

// increase your pace
// encounter a hill or another force that creates resistance
// run long enough to exhaust the slow-twitch fibers

Depending on their fitness level, some runners can go an hour at a modest pace before they begin to recruit the fast-twitch fibers; others can go as much as twice that long. Depending on how fast you are, you may rely on Type I fibers almost exclusively during your half-marathon. If you are on the course for a longer period, however, those fibers will begin to tire, and your body will begin to employ the Type IIa fibers, those slightly larger, aerobic, fast-twitch fibers. If you've trained properly, you'll have enough leeway to get through the rest of your race using these fibers. They aren't great for endurance running, but they are a good substitute for the exhausted Type I fibers. Issues arise when the undertrained runner is forced to go to the third line of defense: Type IIb fibers. Remember, these are built for power, and they fatigue quickly. If you are relying on these fibers to get to the finish, things will not end well.

What the Hansons Method seeks to do is teach you how to maximize the use of the Type I and Type IIa muscle fibers, without having to resort to the Type IIb fibers.

VO$_2$max: Second in command

If muscle fibers are in the driver's seat when it comes to endurance potential, then VO$_2$max works in the pit, constantly providing assistance. VO$_2$max stands for "volume of oxygen uptake," defined as the body's maximum capacity to transport and utilize oxygen while running. When a person's VO$_2$max is 50/ml/kg/min, it is read "50 milliliters of oxygen per kilogram of body weight per minute." What you really need to know is that the higher the number, the better. Although VO$_2$max is often considered the gold standard of fitness, it doesn't always serve as the best predictor of running performance. In fact, elite marathon runners tend to have a slightly lower VO$_2$max than elite 5K and 10K runners. Still, though it isn't the single most important predictor of your racing potential, it remains a significant piece of the puzzle. Generally speaking, faster half-marathon runners tend to have a slightly higher VO$_2$max than slower runners because, as discussed, the slower runners tend to adapt more like a marathon runner in terms of fat utilization and fiber type, and they have slightly lower VO_2max levels. VO_2max will improve with training. Thus, slower runners can improve their VO_2max—and thus their performance—with an increase in training. Let's examine this more closely.

VO_2max is the maximal rate at which oxygen can be brought in and used by exercising muscle.

Because blood carries oxygen to the muscles, one must look at the heart when considering VO_2max. Like the skeletal muscles, the heart muscle can be strengthened with work, thus allowing it to pump more blood and deliver more oxygen to the muscles. The heart adapts to training stress in the same way the muscles in your legs do. Consider the positive adaptations related to the heart that occur as a result of endurance training. Four of these adaptations, shown in Figure 2.1 and described below, are considered the central components of VO_2max:

CIRCULATION OF THE CORONARY ARTERIES IMPROVES // Improved circulation means more blood reaches the heart.

VENTRICLE WALLS THICKEN, PARTICULARLY THE LEFT VENTRICLE // As these thicken, the force of the contractions becomes greater, pumping more blood into the circulating arteries.

THE CHAMBER OF THE VENTRICLE BECOMES LARGER // This allows for more oxygenated blood to be stored within the ventricle, which is then circulated throughout the body.

PULSE DECREASES // When the cardiac muscle is strengthened, it doesn't have to work as hard to do its job.

In sum, more blood is pumped with greater force and less effort. Because the heart has bigger chambers that hold more blood, heart rate slows across all running paces, making the entire system more efficient and healthier.

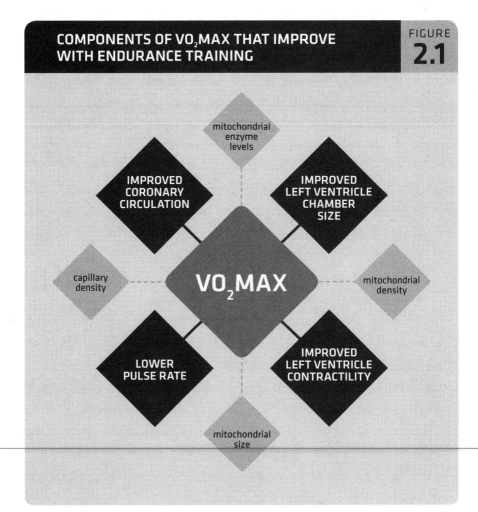

COMPONENTS OF VO$_2$MAX THAT IMPROVE WITH ENDURANCE TRAINING

FIGURE
2.1

mitochondrial enzyme levels

IMPROVED CORONARY CIRCULATION

IMPROVED LEFT VENTRICLE CHAMBER SIZE

capillary density

VO$_2$MAX

mitochondrial density

LOWER PULSE RATE

IMPROVED LEFT VENTRICLE CONTRACTILITY

mitochondrial size

The heart supplies blood to the body, and the better it can deliver large amounts of blood into the bloodstream, the more efficiently the oxygen in the blood reaches the running muscles. What's more, the adaptations don't stop with the heart; they also affect the blood itself. Indeed, blood volume has been shown to increase with endurance training. Red blood cells, the most common type of blood cells, are the main means through which oxygen is delivered within the human body. With endurance training, the hematocrit level, the amount of red blood cells within the total volume of blood, decreases. This means that since total blood volume is higher and the blood itself is less viscous, it can travel through the heart and arteries with much greater ease. Think of the difference between new oil that has just been put in your car and the gunk that's been sitting in the engine for the last 15,000 miles. A lower hematocrit level equates to less wear and tear on your system because, as the red blood cells become larger with training, you lose less oxygen-carrying capacity. Although it may sound counterproductive, since plasma volume increases, the hematocrit level decreases because it is expressed as a percentage of volume. So even though the percentage is lower, the total number of red blood cells can be higher. Remember, 20 percent of 100 equals 20 red blood cells, and 20 percent of 500 equals 100 red blood cells, giving you more bang for your buck.

With endurance training, the heart becomes a stronger pump, and the blood supply becomes bigger and better, but none of that matters if the muscles cannot use the massive amount of oxygen that is now being dropped off at their doorstep. The actual delivery of oxygen to the muscles happens in the capillary bed, which is the end of the line for the artery. Some of these capillaries are so small that only one red blood cell can drop off its bounty of oxygen to the muscle at a time. From there, the red blood cell begins its journey back to the heart and lungs, where it is reloaded with oxygen. During rest, many of these capillary lines lie dormant. As you begin running, the lines open up, allowing muscles to accept an increasing amount of oxygen to meet the demands of exercise.

While improving the central components of VO$_2$max is important, having a bigger left ventricle to pump more blood doesn't do much good if the muscles that are being used can't handle the changes. Luckily, our running muscles, as we discussed, adapt simultaneously. Some of the key peripheral components that we see through endurance training, as shown in Figure 2.1, are the following:

INCREASED CAPILLARY DENSITY // A larger density of capillaries means that oxygen can exchange cells faster and more efficiently, the end result being that the exercising muscle gets the oxygen it needs to continue to exercise.

IMPROVED MITOCHONDRIAL ENZYME LEVELS AND ACTIVITY // Think of enzymes as tools that make work easier. They reduce the amount of energy required to make a reaction occur. With higher levels, reactions within the mitochondria can allow more work to be done at the same rate.

IMPROVED MITOCHONDRIAL DENSITY // The mitochondria are where fats and carbohydrates are presented as fuel for exercise, so the more mitochondria we have, the more fat that can be used as fuel to maintain aerobic intensity.

INCREASED SIZE OF EXISTING MITOCHONDRIA // Bigger mitochondria allow more fuel to be processed at a single site. If we can process more fatty acids through bigger and more mitochondria, we reduce the need for carbohydrates to be used and increase the needed intensity it takes to prompt the anaerobic system (reliance on carbohydrates for energy).

The bottom line is that the body is remarkable at adapting to training. It will do everything it can to support a given activity and become better at it. VO_2max is the ceiling for your aerobic potential, but it is not the overall determinant of potential performance. When your aerobic capacities become maxed out, your anaerobic faculties are right on their heels. As a result, other physiological variables contribute to how well a person can run a half-marathon.

Although it isn't necessary to determine your VO_2max, and we can guarantee the number will climb with additional endurance training, it is a great indicator of progress. There are a number of ways to figure out your VO_2max, some more expensive than others. On the high-precision and high-cost end of the spectrum, you can visit your local gym and have your capacity tested with an array of fancy equipment. This will require you to run on a treadmill with a breathing tube, increasing your speed incrementally. Twenty minutes and $100 later, you'll have a printout with some cold, hard data. For a similar experience but potentially less cost, look into signing up to be a guinea pig at your local university's exercise physiology lab. Graduate students often can provide you with a wealth of information, and you usually won't have to shell out a dime. I am a believer in lab testing for the sake of improvement, provided the feedback is of practical use to you. What good are numbers if you can't apply them? Both as an athlete and as a coach, when I look at VO_2max and thresholds, I am only interested in whether they show improvement. Unfortunately, the results of exercise lab tests often omit the corresponding paces for these levels and thresholds. For example, when you get tested, the technician will often give you a number such as 50 ml/kg/min and tell you whether that is good, average, or below average. That's great, but how do I use that information? What does it mean for me? If you choose to be tested, try to obtain the paces at which you are reaching certain physiological levels. You can then translate that information directly into your training paces.

If you're not interested in getting rigged up to a machine, consider doing a field test. I use the Balke test, for which you need only a track, a stopwatch, and a calculator. Although the equation can vary slightly, the following is used by well-known running coach Dr. Joe Vigil, an expert in the world of running science:

$$VO_2max = 0.178 \times ([m \div 15] - 150) + 33.3$$

We solve this equation by completing the Balke test. To complete the test, do a thorough warm-up and follow these steps:

1. On the track, run fast for 15 minutes, covering as much distance as possible. (Remember to pace yourself. Don't run as hard as you can from the start, but rather build into it, so that you can be running the fastest over the last few minutes.)
2. Convert the distance you have run into meters. To do this, multiply the number of laps by 400 meters (1 lap = 400 meters on a standard track).
3. Take the number in meters and convert it to meters per minute by dividing it by 15 (the number of minutes you ran).
4. Take the number from step 3 and subtract the first 150 m.
5. The remaining number is then multiplied by 0.178 and added to the base of 33.3. Note: If you don't have a speed of greater than

CONTINUES ↘

↘ CONTINUED

150 m/min, take the difference between your speed and 150, multiply by 0.178, and subtract that number from the base of 33.3.

For example, we want to solve for this equation:

$$VO_2max = 0.178 \times ([m \div 15] - 150) + 33.3$$

Our runner completes the test, covering 10 laps in 15 minutes. He converts laps to meters and replaces the "m" with a number:

$$10 \text{ laps} \times 400 \text{ m/lap} = 4000 \text{ m}$$

The equation now looks like this:

$$VO_2max = 0.178 ([4000 \div 15] - 150) + 33.3$$

Next, the runner solves within the brackets:

$$[4000 \div 15] \text{ or } 266.67$$

Now the equation looks like this:

$$VO_2max = 0.178 (266.67 - 150) + 33.3$$

Finally, the runner simply solves the equation:

$$VO_2max = 0.178 (116.67) + 33.3$$

$$VO_2max = 20.77 + 33.3$$

$$VO_2max = 54 \text{ or, more precisely, } 54 \text{ ml/kg/min}$$

This means that our runner's current aerobic fitness is 54.

After determining your baseline VO_2max, you can repeat this test in the middle of your training to check your progress. Keep in mind that the more advanced the runner, the fewer changes are seen. What can always change, however, even if only slightly, is the pace you can run at your VO_2max. That's what really matters in the end.

Anaerobic threshold: Power player

As discussed previously, long-distance running relies heavily on the oxygen supplied by the aerobic system, which is more efficient and provides greater endurance than the anaerobic system. The anaerobic system is powerful and explosive, but it functions without oxygen and therefore can provide only short bursts of speed before energy stores are depleted, lactic acid builds up in the muscles, and running ceases. While lactic acid, or lactate, has gotten a bad rap as a soreness-inducing, fatigue-causing by-product of high-intensity exercise, it actually serves as an energy source for the muscles, allowing them to squeak out a bit more work before bonking. Research now tells us that the fatigue that occurs at that point is caused by another physiological phenomenon. The real culprits are the electrolytes—sodium, potassium, and calcium— that are positioned along the muscles, each with its own electrical charge that triggers muscle contractions. At high intensities and over time, the potassium ion outside the cell builds up and cannot switch places with the sodium ion inside the cell. This leads to weaker and weaker muscle contractions, a condition called neuromuscular fatigue, meaning your body will soon slow to a sputtering halt.

Not only is blood lactate not the villain we once thought it to be, but we've also come to see that it plays a key role in distance running. The aerobic system supports a moderate pace for long periods because the lactate that is produced is simultaneously processed and removed.

However, as the aerobic system fatigues or the intensity increases, you become more dependent on the anaerobic system and, in turn, reach a point where you produce lactate faster than your body can get rid of it. Referred to as lactate threshold, onset of blood lactate, or anaerobic threshold, this is the tipping point at which lactic acid starts to build up in your bloodstream.

> **anaerobic threshold** is the pace at which lactic acid will begin to accumulate exponentially, despite running at a steady pace.

Anaerobic threshold is particularly important because it has been identified as perhaps the best predictor of endurance performance. It occurs at anywhere between 60 and 90 percent or more of a person's VO_2max, so as you get closer to your VO_2max, blood lactate begins to accumulate. The best of the best tend to have an anaerobic threshold exceeding 70 percent of VO_2max. Training may raise your VO_2max only a few points, but it can have a significant impact on anaerobic threshold. If you look at a group of elite marathon runners, their VO_2max levels will be similar; what tends to separate 1st place from 10th place is anaerobic threshold. While VO_2max may separate the national class from recreational runners, anaerobic threshold separates the champions from the contenders.

As with VO_2max, testing your anaerobic threshold is always an option, but it requires some guesswork unless you have the testing done in a fancy lab, with the numbers printed out for you. Our advice is to see how your body responds to the workouts on the plan. As mentioned, anaerobic threshold pace can be maintained for about an hour. If you don't have these paces to use, then ask yourself, "Can I hold this for an hour straight?" Adjust your pace accordingly based on your response.

Remember that anaerobic threshold is the point at which the aerobic pathways are still providing energy for muscle contraction, but they can't do it fast enough to provide all the required energy. This is where the anaerobic pathways begin to make up the difference. As a rule of thumb, a person can run at his or her anaerobic threshold for about an hour. As you may have guessed, this becomes increasingly important for elite runners, whose half-marathon times tend to hover around an hour. For these folks, having a high anaerobic threshold is probably more important than being able to burn fat for fuel. The higher this threshold is, the faster they can cover the distance before having to slow down; thus, raising this level is critical for their individual success. For slower runners, anaerobic threshold may be a better representation of their 10K times because their 10K times probably hover closer to that 1-hour mark than do their half-marathon times. So, although anaerobic threshold is important for slower runners (and even more so as they become faster), the ability to burn fat and save glycogen will probably have more bearing on their success.

We can push the threshold higher via training. By running farther and faster, we train our bodies to rely more heavily on the aerobic pathways, thus improving endurance and increasing the time it takes to reach the point of anaerobic reliance. One of the big differences between the Hansons Method and traditional training programs is that we teach you to stimulate aerobic metabolism through a large volume of aerobic training, not high-end anaerobic work.

Aerobic threshold: Glycogen depletion

All this talk about energy systems may have you wondering where that energy comes from in the first place. The short answer: fats and carbohydrates. As an endurance runner, you should focus on training the body to use fat as the primary source of energy. Our bodies store very small amounts of carbohydrates for quick energy, but our fat stores are nearly endless. Even if you have only a small percentage of body fat, your system has plenty of fat for fuel. Fat is particularly high in energy because it provides nearly twice as many calories per gram as do carbohydrates. The only problem is that the oxidation of fat to energy is slower than the oxidation of carbohydrates. For most people, fat serves as the main source of energy for up to about 50 percent of VO_2max because up to that point the fat can be processed fast enough through the mitochondria to supply the demands that running requires. For most runners, however, 50 percent of VO_2max is painfully slow. After that point, whether as a result of distance or intensity, the body looks to burn carbohydrates. The term *aerobic threshold* reflects the pace at which the proportion of fat and carbohydrate being used for fuel is about 50/50. See Figure 2.2 for a graph that illustrates the contribution of fat and carbohydrate based on running intensity.

aerobic threshold is considered the pace at which fats and carbohydrates are being consumed at approximately the same rate (50/50).

The reason carbohydrates (glycogen) provide the majority of energy at faster paces is because fat is metabolized slower than carbohydrate. The downside of relying on glycogen stores for energy is that you have only about 2 hours' worth, and once they are gone, your run is over. When you burn through your stored glycogen, your body will draw upon the glucose in your blood, which runs out even more

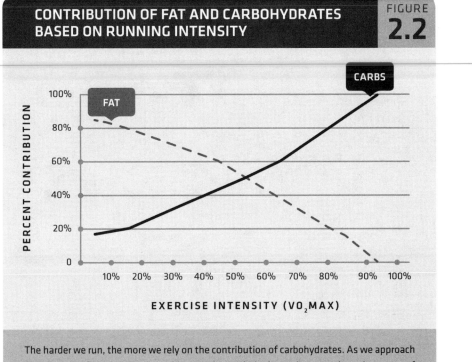

CONTRIBUTION OF FAT AND CARBOHYDRATES BASED ON RUNNING INTENSITY

FIGURE **2.2**

The harder we run, the more we rely on the contribution of carbohydrates. As we approach 100 percent of our maximal aerobic capacity, carbohydrates become the sole source of energy, making carbohydrates the limiting factor in exercise duration and intensity.

quickly. The result is "hitting the wall" or "bonking." While bonking is more common during a full marathon, poorly prepared or poorly fueled runners can certainly experience it in the half-marathon distance. How do you know if you have hit the wall? For one, your pace slows perceptibly, and the feeling associated with bonking has been described as similar to dragging a 300-pound anchor behind you. Although this was once thought to be an unavoidable rite of passage for long-distance racers, a smart training plan will help you skirt the wall altogether. It's all about burning fat for a longer time to put off drawing on those limited carbohydrate stores.

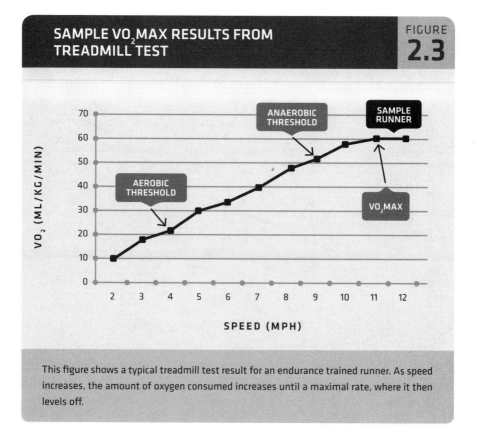

SAMPLE VO$_2$MAX RESULTS FROM TREADMILL TEST

FIGURE
2.3

This figure shows a typical treadmill test result for an endurance trained runner. As speed increases, the amount of oxygen consumed increases until a maximal rate, where it then levels off.

Being able to "burn" fat more efficiently is invaluable across the spectrum of paces. Faster runners are running at a high percentage of their VO$_2$max for a significant amount of time, and a larger proportion of their energy expenditure is coming from the use of carbohydrates. So, even though they are likely to finish the half-marathon in less than 2 hours, they can still nearly exhaust their stores because the percentage of glycogen usage is so high. Meanwhile, those on the slower end of the spectrum are out on the course for more than 2 hours, and being able to utilize fat better will save their glycogen stores and ensure that they can complete the race and even finish strong.

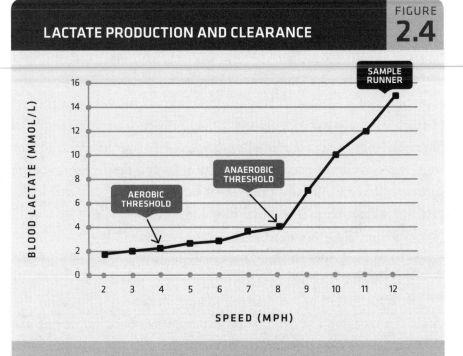

LACTATE PRODUCTION AND CLEARANCE

FIGURE **2.4**

A blood lactate test shows more clearly the deflection points at the same intensities as the VO₂max test. At about 4 mph, there is the first increase in blood lactate, indicating the increased reliance on carbohydrates. At 8 mph, there is the second, more exponential, increase, indicating the inability for lactate clearance to match lactate production.

Luckily for the distance runner, it is possible to train the body to burn fat longer. The speed at which fat can be processed doesn't change with training, so to be able to use more fat, we have to burn a higher volume of it. To do this, we need more metabolic factories (the mitochondria, which, as mentioned earlier, are the powerhouse of the cell). Aerobic training, such as running, helps to increase the number of mitochondria, which in turn introduces new enzyme activity and oxygen to the system. While the mitochondria are not necessarily producing more quickly, they are bigger and more plentiful, which allows fat to be oxidized and turned into energy for muscle contraction. With the increase in energy from fat, the glycogen in the muscles isn't tapped until later, saving it for faster paces. Basically, the wall is pushed back and, with any luck, never reached.

Figures 2.3 and 2.4 illustrate what has been discussed so far. Figure 2.3 represents typical results of a VO_2max treadmill test of a trained runner. For the most part, as the intensity increases, you observe a linear increase in the amount of oxygen used. At our threshold points, we can see slight deflections on the graph. The first represents the aerobic threshold; the second represents the anaerobic threshold. Figure 2.4 represents the actual blood lactate measurements from a treadmill test. By graphing the amount of lactate in the blood at set intervals of a test, we can again see the deflection points that coincide with our threshold points.

The take-home here is that improving one's aerobic threshold is vital for a successful half-marathon, regardless of pace. Improving the ability to process fat as a fuel at higher intensities will give you more stamina and ultimately make you faster. From a training perspective it shows why easy runs, which are a large part of the Hansons Method, facilitate quality adaptations in the short term and long term. They are far from "junk miles" and should not be omitted.

Running economy: Pace matters

Running economy, which describes how much oxygen is required to run a certain pace, is the final physiological topic runners should understand. Consider this scenario: Runner A and Runner B both have the same VO_2max of 60 ml/kg/min. It might take Runner B 50 ml/kg/min to run a 6:30 mile, while it takes Runner A 55 ml/kg/min to run the same pace. Given this, Runner B is more economical than Runner A but, more important, is probably faster too. See Figure 2.5 for a graphic example.

running economy is the amount of oxygen a runner utilizes to run a certain pace. The less oxygen required, the better.

Although there has been much debate over the effects of running economy, two facts are clear. First, running economy depends on a high training volume. You don't need to pound out 120-mile weeks, but your mileage should be sufficient for the distance for which you

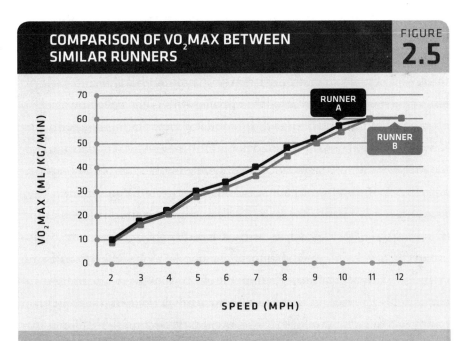

COMPARISON OF VO$_2$MAX BETWEEN SIMILAR RUNNERS

FIGURE **2.5**

The difference between beating your rivals or losing to them can be a matter of running economy. This figure shows that Runner A and Runner B have similar VO$_2$max numbers, but Runner B uses slightly less oxygen at any given speed. This means Runner A is working a little bit harder than Runner B, and that may be the difference in winning or losing.

are training. When I say "sufficient," I am referring to the amount of mileage required to perform well in your event. For instance, 20 miles a week is sufficient volume for a beginning 5K runner but not nearly enough for an advanced half-marathoner. This varies depending on the event you are training for, the number of months and years you have been running, and how fast you are attempting to run.

The second component of running economy is speed training. By training at a certain pace, you become more economical at that pace. Because the goal is to improve running economy at race pace, you must spend an adequate amount of time training at race pace. This also underscores why it is important not to run workouts faster than prescribed and why pace is such a key part of our program. When you opt to run faster than suggested, you are training at a level that you may not be ready for, based on actual race performances. Training above suggested paces turns workouts into something they were not intended to be; for example, easy runs may now resemble tempo runs, tempo runs become strength runs, and strength runs become speed runs. These paces may feel achievable at first, but it is our experience that the majority of people who train too fast end up overtrained, burned-out, or injured. If you feel strongly about training at a faster pace, then it is important to run (or simulate) a race to confirm that you are ready to move to a more aggressive pace goal.

The validity of running economy is not without some controversy. Some coaches and well-known exercise science folks question whether running economy matters when comparing runners. If the runners are comparable in race times, then maybe it does. If they are not, it may not really matter. Put another way, if you are a construction worker looking to buy a new pickup, do you care about the economy of a coupe? Probably not, because it's not what you want to buy. But if you find you can get a new F150 that gets 30 miles per gallon without a loss in performance, your ears perk up, right? This is especially so if the truck outperforms others on the market. What I am saying is, economy is important, but use it as a way to evaluate your own personal improvement. If you improve your running economy, then you are going to get faster. If you process fat better and improve your VO_2max and your anaerobic threshold, you will be a better runner. And because of these improvements, you will be able to run faster using less energy. For instance, prior to training, perhaps you ran 7:00 minutes per mile and were at 75 percent VO_2max, and now you are running the same pace but at 70 percent VO_2max. Running economy allows you to quantify such changes and gives you a look at how these factors have helped you to improve.

A physiologically based method

By understanding the physiological factors involved in optimal endurance training, you can understand the justification for each workout. As muscle fibers adapt to running stress, VO_2max is optimized, anaerobic threshold improves, and the ability to burn fat at higher intensities increases. In the end, improved running economy is the result of consistent, optimal training. It all comes down to the tiny biological happenings of the human body; increased capillarization, an increased number and size of mitochondria, and greater mitochondrial enzyme activity equate to less oxygen being needed to run the same paces. The beauty of the Hansons Method is that it allows runners of all abilities to do the same workouts but at paces that are going to benefit the individual. The physiological adaptations are what make you better, and the Hansons Method is designed to ensure you develop these adaptations.

PART II

the
program

3

Training program components

I RECENTLY HAD A conversation with one of our coaches regarding success. He asked me, "Is it considered a success when a runner does 50 percent of the work and achieves 70 percent of his goal?" The question arose when one of our online athletes spent an entire training segment struggling to find any semblance of consistency. Workouts were constantly being changed, moved, or abandoned. By the end of this athlete's training block, we were wondering how well a runner could do when a training plan was so drastically altered. Well, we got that answer. Unfortunately, for our athlete, it was not a good result.

In Chapter 2, we discussed the unique physiology of the half-marathon and how individual it can be. In this chapter, we will examine the components of training that will take that complex physiology and turn it into a formula that will get you to your half-marathon goal.

As you begin to dissect our training plans, consider the various elements that make up the Just Finish Program, the Beginner Program, and the Advanced Program. By varying your training from one day to the next, you train different systems, which all work in concert to optimize your running potential. Runs are organized in categories: easy days and something of substance (SOS) workouts. Figure 3.1 shows the breakdown of weekly mileage. The SOS workouts include long, tempo, strength, and speed runs. Long runs are included under SOS because, by definition, they require more effort than a regular easy day. However, their pace is slower than race pace and could be defined as easy. Specifically, long run pace in half-marathon training is 1:10–2:30 per mile slower than your race pace.

Often, we are asked about incorporating hills, or hill repeats, in training. As you may notice, the training program has no specific designation of hills. In part this is to simplify the program and make it easy to follow. Hills are a great aspect of training, but for the purposes of our book and our audience, they may be better dealt with on an individual basis. Additionally, training for any endurance event should involve training on a variety of surfaces. In particular, while speed workouts are usually done on a track or flat area, strength workouts should be done on more undulating terrain. For instance, the Hansons-Brooks Distance Project athletes do strength workouts on a 6-mile loop at a local park that includes rolling terrain. This allows them to experience hills during an SOS workout without having to devote specific workouts to hills.

the overload principle is the idea that regular exposure to a specific exercise will enhance certain physiological functions and therefore induce a training response. (You become more fit.)

The basis for the Hansons Method's varied approach stems from the overload principle, which states that when the body engages in an activity that disrupts its present state of homeostasis (inner balance), certain

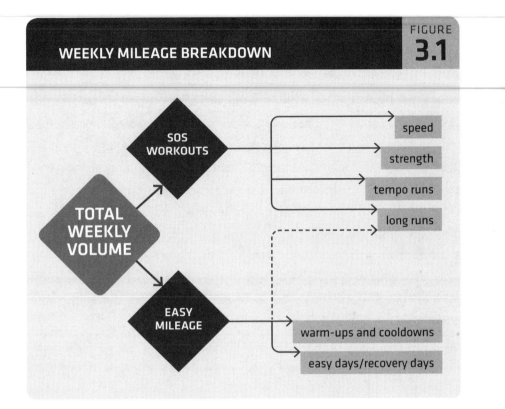

FIGURE 3.1

WEEKLY MILEAGE BREAKDOWN

recovery mechanisms are initiated. As discussed in Chapter 2, different stresses work to overload the system, stimulating physiological changes. These adaptations, in turn, better prepare the body for that particular stress the next time it is encountered. This is where the principle of cumulative fatigue comes in, which underscores our entire training philosophy. Cumulative fatigue is all about challenging the body without reaching the point of no return (overtraining). Over the course of training, you'll notice that our workouts are designed to stress the different thresholds without maxing out any single one. By doing the various workouts at the prescribed pace and intensity, you will walk that line right to the edge for maximum benefits, but never cross over it.

Easy days

EASY RUNNING

Misconceptions abound when it comes to easy running. Such training is often thought of as unnecessary, filler mileage. Many new runners believe that these days can be considered optional because they don't provide any real benefits. Don't be fooled; easy mileage plays a vital role in a runner's development. Every run doesn't need to be—and should not be—a knock-down, drag-out experience. Easy runs dole out plenty of important advantages, without any of the pain, by providing a gentler overload that can be applied in a higher volume than in SOS workouts. This keeps the body in a constant state of slight disruption, protecting you from getting injured while simultaneously forcing your body to adapt to stress to increase fitness.

In the Advanced Program's peak week, we prescribe a ceiling of 50 miles (give or take a couple miles). If we look closer, 30 of those miles, or 60 percent, are classified as easy. This figure includes the long run, because even though the distance of the run can make it an SOS day, the benefits you gain from the long run are the same as what you gain from easy runs. Figure 3.2 provides justification for why nearly half of the weekly mileage is devoted to this type of training.

To understand why easy running is important, you must consider the physiological adaptations that it stimulates in muscle fiber development, energy utilization, capillary development, cardiovascular strength, and structural fitness.

Physiology of easy running

When considering reasons why easy running is important, look no further than what it does for the muscle fibers. As discussed in Chapter 2, even though the amount of slow-twitch fibers a runner is geneti-

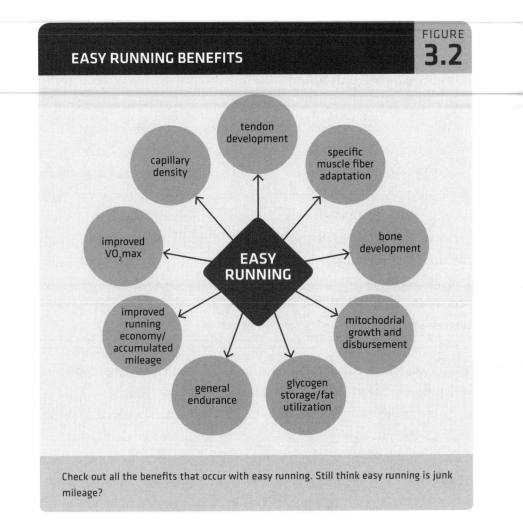

FIGURE 3.2

EASY RUNNING BENEFITS

Check out all the benefits that occur with easy running. Still think easy running is junk mileage?

cally endowed with will ultimately define his or her potential as a half-marathoner, training can make a difference. Easy running recruits a whole host of slow-twitch fibers because they have a lower "firing," or contraction, threshold than the more powerful fast-twitch fibers. Like any other muscle, the more they are used, the more they develop. Along with improved resistance to fatigue, slow-twitch muscles can be relied upon for more miles, keeping the fast-twitch muscles from being fully engaged until farther down the road. In the end, easy running helps develop slow-twitch fibers that are more fatigue-resistant and fast-twitch fibers that take on many of the characteristics of the slow-twitch fibers.

What's more, the more slow-twitch fibers you have, the better you'll be prepared to use fats for energy. We now know this is a very good thing because the body contains copious amounts of fat to burn and only a limited supply of carbohydrates. The greater length of time you burn fat, rather than carbohydrate, the longer you put off encountering the dreaded "wall" as a result of glycogen (carbohydrate) depletion. When you run at lower intensities, you burn around 70 percent fat and 30 percent carbohydrate. With an increase in pace comes an increase in the percentage of carbohydrates you burn. Your easy running days serve as catalysts to develop those slow-twitch muscle fibers and, consequently, teach your body to burn fats over carbohydrates. Slow-twitch fibers are better than fast-twitch fibers at burning fat because they contain greater amounts of mitochondria, enzymes that burn fat, and capillaries.

In response to the need for fat to provide the lion's share of the fuel for training, the mitochondria grow larger and are dispersed throughout the muscles. In fact, research has indicated that just six to seven months of training can spur the mitochondria to grow in size by as much as 35 percent and in number by 5 percent. This benefits you as a runner because the higher density of mitochondria works to break down fat more effectively. For instance, if you burned 60 percent fat at a certain pace a year ago, training may have increased that percentage to 70 percent.

Thanks to easy running, your body will also see an uptick in the enzymes that help to burn fat. Every cell in your body contains these enzymes, which sit waiting to be "turned on" by aerobic activity. No pills or special surgeries are needed; this is simply your body's natural way of burning fat. The enzymes work to make it possible for fats to enter the bloodstream and then travel to the muscles to be used as fuel. With the help of the increased mitochondria and fat-burning enzymes, the body utilizes fat for a longer period, pushing back "the wall" and keeping you running longer.

Capillary development is another benefit of easy running. Because running requires a greater amount of blood to supply oxygen to your system, the number of capillaries within the exercising muscles increases with training. After just a few months of running, capillary beds can increase by as much as 40 percent. In addition, slow-twitch fibers contain a more extensive network of capillaries than do fast-twitch fibers, supplying those slower fibers with much more oxygen. As the density of capillaries increases throughout those muscles, a greater amount of oxygen is supplied in a more efficient manner.

Easy running also results in a number of adaptations that happen outside the exercising muscles. As you know, your body requires more oxygen as workload increases, and the way to deliver more oxygen to your system is to deliver more blood. With several months of training, much of which is easy running, a runner will experience an increase in hemoglobin, the "oxygen transporter," in addition to a 35–40 percent increase in plasma volume. This increased volume not only helps deliver oxygen but also carries away the waste products that result from metabolism.

The best way to encourage these developments is through easy running. If a person were to eliminate the easy runs from a program, all these adaptations would be greatly reduced. On the one hand, think about the volume of running you can do in an interval workout; it might be just a few miles of hard work. On the other hand, think about the amount of easy running you can do—miles and miles per week. When you try to stress a system at the top (near 100 percent of capability), you can do only a limited amount of work. When you build a system from the bottom up, you can do a much larger volume. In other words, your daily easy runs provide the heart a much bigger opportunity to adapt to a moderate workload, rather than a limited volume of extremely hard work.

Easy running also leads to certain structural changes to your physiological system that are advantageous for good running of any distance. The main adaptation occurs within the tendons of the running muscles. During running, the body lands at a force several times that of the runner's body weight; the faster the pace, the greater that force becomes. The resulting strain on tendons and joints, applied gradually through easy running, allows the body to slowly adapt to higher-impact forces so it can later handle the greater demands of fast-paced running.

Collectively, these adaptations stimulated by easy running prompt improvements in VO_2max, anaerobic threshold, and running economy. Whereas fast anaerobic workouts provide little improvement in the muscles' aerobic capacity and endurance, large amounts of easy running can bump aerobic development upward by leaps and bounds. Whether you're looking to strengthen your heart, transport more oxygen to the working muscles, or simply be able to run longer at a certain pace, all signs point to the benefit of including a good deal of easy running in your training.

Easy running guidelines

An easy run is usually defined as one that lasts anywhere between 20 minutes and 2.5 hours at an intensity of 55–75 percent of VO_2max. Because most of us don't have the means to get VO_2max tested, the next best thing is to look at pace per mile. The Hansons Half-Marathon Method calls for easy runs to be paced 1:30–2:30 minutes slower than goal race pace. For example, if your goal half-marathon pace is 7:00 minutes per mile, your easy pace should be 8:30–9:30 minutes per mile. While easy running is a necessary part of training, and controlling your pace is key to its effectiveness, be sure not to run *too* easy. If your pace is excessively slow, you are simply breaking down tendon and bone without obtaining any aerobic benefits. Refer to Table 3.5 at the end of this chapter for your specific guidelines.

Keep in mind that there is a time for "fast" easy runs (1:30 minutes per mile slower than half-marathon pace) and also a time for "slow" easy runs (2:30 minutes per mile slower than half-marathon pace). "Fast" and "slow" easy runs are not denoted on the calendar, in order to allow for some flexibility depending on your experience and fitness levels. If you are a rookie runner, focus more on covering ground and less on running at a certain speed. Advanced runners, in contrast, should alternate between faster and slower paces for their easy runs, especially during long runs. Warm-ups and cooldowns are instances when you will want to run on the slower end of the spectrum. Here the idea is to simply bridge the gap between no running and fast running and vice versa. The day after an SOS workout is another time you may choose (depending on your experience) a pace on the slow side. For instance, if you have a long run on Sunday and a strength workout on Tuesday, then your Monday run should be easier to ensure you are recovered and ready for a good workout on Tuesday. By running the easy runs on the slower end of the range, beginning runners will safely make the transition to higher mileage. More advanced runners will likely find that they can handle the faster end of the easy range, even after SOS workouts. The day following a tempo run and the second easy day prior to a long run both provide good chances to run closer to 1:30 minutes per mile slower than half-marathon race pace.

Whether you are a novice or an experienced runner looking for a new approach, stick to the plan when it comes to easy running. Have fun with the easy days, allowing yourself to take in the scenery or enjoy a social run with friends. Meanwhile, you'll be simultaneously racking up a laundry list of physiological benefits. What's more, after a nice,

TABLE
3.1
HOW EASY RUNS FIT INTO THE BIG PICTURE

MON*	TUES	WED	THURS
easy	speed	off	tempo
easy	speed	off	tempo
easy	speed	off	tempo

*Monday and Friday pacing should be treated carefully and sensibly.

relaxed run, your body will be clamoring for a challenge, ready to tackle the next SOS workout.

The schedule in Table 3.1 gives you a general idea of how easy runs fit into the overall training schedule. On Mondays, distances will range from 4 to 8 miles, followed by a speed session on Tuesday and then a longer run on Sunday. Also, note that the easy days that land on Fridays follow the Thursday tempo runs. This is where overtraining can occur, when easy runs are sandwiched between SOS workouts. It is common for this to happen during the first part of the training schedules when runners are still feeling fresh, causing them to run faster than prescribed. Remember, these are not the days to worry about how fast you are running; time on your feet is the focus, not pace.

For the Saturday easy run, you can be a little more flexible with pace. If you feel good, run on the faster end of your easy running spectrum. The metabolic adaptations will happen throughout the pace range, but injury can occur if you make a habit of always running faster, so be sure to moderate your pace. Table 3.1 also shows that you get to a point where it is not logical to keep adding workouts to your training week; if progression is to take place, it must come from adding another easy day (Wednesday) and/or adding mileage to the easy days, not from

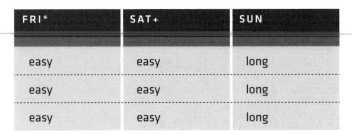

FRI*	SAT+	SUN
easy	easy	long
easy	easy	long
easy	easy	long

+Saturday is a day to consider the faster side of your easy pace range.

simply running harder. You will notice in the Hansons Half-Marathon Method that once the workouts peak in mileage, the easy days are what add to the weekly mileage.

CROSSTRAINING AS A RUNNING SUBSTITUTE

Crosstraining as supplemental training will be discussed in Chapter 7. However, here I would like to address crosstraining serving as replacement training. The Hansons Method is designed to get you to your goal, and that means following the programs as written, as closely as possible. The more you become familiar with our training methods, the more you realize that our programs ask for more running than some other popular training plans. Why? Because to get better at running, you need to run. This is called "specificity." Exchanging easy runs for crosstraining workouts takes away a vital component of running development and the concomitant physiological developments and benefits discussed in this chapter. It also sets the runner up for a potential downfall in races. Why? Programs that specify less running and fewer running days per week tend to produce runners who are always fresh for workouts; thus, these athletes tend to run the workouts too hard yet feel good doing it. This can lead to overconfidence and poor strategy on race day. One of the primary arguments I get from the runners I coach is "But, Luke, I can't run mileage. I always get hurt." Instead, they prefer a 3-day-a-week program, adding in crosstraining on other days of the week. This is not going to get you to your best half-marathon. You do not need to be afraid of mileage; most people can handle increases in mileage when they are done in a gradual manner. But you do need to add mileage the right way:

// Don't go from all crosstraining to all running. Phase out crosstraining gradually. Try replacing a crosstraining session with a run each week, prior to beginning our training program.

// Consider adding mileage to your shorter runs little by little, such as simply adding a mile to each of your easy runs during the week.

// Run your appropriate paces, even if it means slowing down, especially for your easy days.

SOS workouts

THE LONG RUN

When it comes to training for distance races, nothing gets more press— good and bad—than the long run. It has become a status symbol among runners in training, a measure by which one compares oneself with one's running counterparts. For many, the long run is like a big question mark, hovering in your training plan, something you aren't sure you'll survive, but you subject yourself to the suffering nonetheless. Although the long run doesn't cast as large a shadow in half-marathon training as it does in marathon training, it remains a focal point for most good half-marathon programs. It is surprising, then, to discover that much of the existing advice on running long is misguided. After relatively low-mileage weeks, some plans suggest grueling long runs that end up more akin to running misadventures than productive training. For example, a 16-mile long run at the end of a 3-day-a-week half-marathon training program can be both demoralizing and injurious.

Our approach to the half-marathon is thoughtful and methodical, with long run mileage chosen in line with the overall goal of achieving cumulative fatigue. For reasons discussed in Chapter 1, cumulative fatigue is key to the Hansons Method's success. However, the long run should successfully stimulate this effect without completely zapping your legs. This way, rather than spending the entire week recovering from the previous long run, you continue to build your base for the forthcoming long effort.

Take a look at a week in the program that includes a Sunday long run (see Table 4.3). Leading up to it, you will do a tempo run on Thursday and easier short runs on Friday and Saturday. We don't give you a day completely off before a long run because recovery occurs on the easy running days. Because no single workout has totally diminished your energy stores and left your legs feeling wrecked, fatigue accumulates over time. The plan allows for partial recovery, but it is designed to keep you from feeling completely fresh going into a long run. Following the Sunday long run, you will have an easy day on Monday and a strength workout on Tuesday. This may initially appear to be too much, but because your long run's pace and mileage are tailored to your ability and experience, less recovery time is needed.

Physiology of long runs

Long runs provide a number of benefits, many of which correlate with the gains from easy running. Mentally, long runs help you build confidence as you increase your mileage from one week to the next. They help you develop the coping skills necessary to complete any endurance event. They teach you how to persist even when you are not feeling 100 percent. Because you never know what is going to happen on race day, this can be a real asset. Most notable, however, are the physiological adaptations that occur as a result of long runs. Improved VO_2max, increased capillary growth, a stronger heart, and the ability to utilize fat on a cellular level are among the benefits. When your body is trained to run long, it adapts and learns to store more glycogen, thereby allowing you to go farther before becoming exhausted.

The benefits of long runs include:

// greater confidence as you increase mileage across weeks
// improved VO_2max
// ability to utilize fat on a cellular level
// increased muscle strength
// increased energy stores in muscles

In addition to increasing the energy stores in your muscles, long runs increase muscle strength. Although your body first exploits the slow-twitch muscle fibers during a long run, it eventually begins to recruit the fast-twitch fibers as the slow-twitch fibers fatigue. The only way to train those fast-twitch fibers is to run long enough to tire the slow-twitch fibers first; by strengthening all of these fibers, you'll avoid bonking on race day. By now the majority of these adaptations are probably starting to sound familiar.

Long run guidelines

Advice from renowned running researcher and coach Dr. Jack Daniels provides a basis for our long run philosophy. He instructs runners never to exceed 25–30 percent of their weekly mileage in a long run, whether they are training for a 5K, a half-marathon, or a full marathon. He adds that a 2:30-hour to 3:00-hour time limit should be enforced, suggesting that exceeding those guidelines offers no physiological benefit and may lead to overtraining, injuries, and burnout. Dr. Dave Martin, running researcher at Georgia State University and a consultant to Team USA, recommends that long runs be between 90 minutes and 2 hours long.

According to legendary South African researcher and author Tim Noakes, a continual easy to moderate run at 70–85 percent VO_2max that is sustained for 2 hours or more will lead to the greatest glycogen depletion. Exercise physiologist Dr. David Costill has also noted that a 2-hour bout of running reduces muscle glycogen by as much as 50 percent. While this rate of glycogen depletion is acceptable on race day, it is counterproductive in the middle of a training cycle because it takes up to 72 hours to replenish these stores. When you diminish your energy stores too dramatically, you can be benched by fatigue, missing out on important training, or you do the training on overly tired legs and end up hurting yourself. Instead of flirting with the point of diminishing returns and prescribing an arbitrary 20-mile run, the Hansons Method looks at percentage of weekly mileage and total time spent running. We determine your long run based on your weekly total mileage and your pace for that long run. It may sound unconventional, but you'll find that nothing we suggest is random; it is firmly based in science, with proven results. Table 3.2 indicates how far your long run should be based on your total mileage for the week.

Pace is a significant part of the equation. In addition to completing the optimal number of miles on each long run, you must adhere to a certain pace to get the most benefit. If you are new to running, or new to running longer distances, the first goal is to simply build your endurance. In that case, running slow enough to be able to cover the distance

TABLE 3.2 LONG RUN DISTANCE BASED ON WEEKLY MILEAGE	25% OF VOLUME	30% OF VOLUME
20 mi./week	5 mi.	6 mi.
30 mi./week	7.5 mi.	9 mi.
40 mi./week	10 mi.	12 mi.
50 mi./week	12.5 mi.	15 mi.

is the objective. As you become more fit, faster, and more experienced, pace begins to play its role in the body's overall adaptations achieved from long runs. As your endurance builds, your pace will probably increase naturally.

Because we don't all cover the same distance in the same amount of time, it only makes sense to adjust a long run depending on how fast you will be traveling. Research tells us that 2–3 hours is the optimal window for metabolic adaptation in terms of long runs. Beyond that window, muscle breakdown begins to occur. Table 3.3 shows how long it takes to complete long runs of 10, 12, and 14 miles, respectively. Making an assumption that slower runners are more likely to be running fewer weekly miles, we can see that these distances are great examples of how mileage, time, and percentage of weekly mileage are all intertwined.

Of course you must first determine the pace you will be running before deciding exactly how long your long runs should be. We generally coach runners to hold an easy to moderate pace throughout a long run. Instead of viewing it as a high-volume easy day, think of it as a long workout. If you are new to the half-marathon, err on the easy side of pacing as you become accustomed to the longer distances. More

TABLE 3.3	LONG RUN DURATIONS BASED ON AVERAGE PACE PER MILE		
PACE/MILE	10 MILES	12 MILES	14 MILES
7:00	1:10:00	1:24:00	1:38:00
8:00	1:20:00	1:36:00	1:52:00
9:00	1:30:00	1:48:00	2:06:00
10:00	1:40:00	2:00:00	2:20:00
11:00	1:50:00	2:12:00	2:34:00
12:00	2:00:00	2:24:00	2:48:00

advanced runners should maintain a moderate pace because their muscles have already adapted to the stress of such feats of endurance. In the big picture of training, when you avoid overdoing these lengthy workouts, you reap more benefits and avoid the potential downfalls of overtraining. Refer to Table 3.5 for exact paces.

SPEED WORKOUTS

With speed workouts, half-marathon training begins to get more interesting. When we refer to speed training, we are talking about interval sessions, also called repeat workouts. Speed workouts require you to run multiple bouts of certain distances at high intensities with recovery between the fast segments. This type of training not only plays a role in prompting some of the important physiological changes we already discussed but also teaches your mind to handle harder work. While easy days are typically low-pressure, speed workouts require you to put your game face on, and discipline is one of many benefits garnered. While you may be able to complete an easy run the morning after a late night out on the town, if you want to get the most out of your speed work, you will need to eat a hearty dinner and hit the hay at a decent hour. For whatever you give up to optimally execute these workouts, the training will give back to you tenfold. Every speed workout you complete is like money in the bank when it comes to resources on which you can draw during the most difficult moments of the race.

Surprisingly, advanced runners often make the same mistakes that novices do in terms of speed training, namely, they neglect it. For instance, we have had runners come to us feeling stale after running several races in a year. Digging into these runners' histories, we often find that they are running so many races that they have completely forgone speed training, spending all their time on long runs, tempo runs, and recovery. Along with flat workouts tend to come stagnated finishing times. That's where we set them straight by guiding them through the Hansons Half-Marathon Method. Like the other types of workouts, speed training is an important part of constantly keeping your system on its toes, requiring it to adapt to workouts that vary in intensity and distance.

Many runners who train for the half-marathon distance have done speed work in the past. Therefore, convincing them that speed work is important is not as difficult as it can be with marathon runners, who tend to neglect it. That said, some folks go too far in the other direction, putting too much emphasis on speed work, which can result in injury. The lesson here is to remember that all training has a purpose and a place.

If you are new to half-marathoning and your past speed workouts have consisted of simply running some days slightly faster than others, you are in the majority. Luckily, the speed workouts we give you here can provide an introductory course on how to implement harder workouts. As you learn to properly implement speed workouts, your training will be transformed from perhaps a somewhat aimless approach to fitness to a guided plan of attack. These workouts can also help you predict what you might be capable of in your half-marathon. With the help of speed work, you can successfully run a shorter race, such as a 5K or 10K, and then plug that time into a race equivalency chart to determine your potential half-marathon time. Additionally, this work helps to highlight weak areas while there is still enough time to address and correct them.

Physiology of speed workouts

The greatest beneficiaries of speed training are the working muscles. With speed sessions, not only the slow-twitch fibers but also the intermediate fibers become maximally activated to provide aerobic energy. This forces the slow-twitch fibers to maximize their aerobic capacities, but it also trains the intermediate fibers to step in when the slow-twitch fibers become fatigued. As a result of better muscle coordination, running economy improves. Stimulated by everything from speed workouts to easy running, running economy is all about how efficiently your body utilizes oxygen at a certain pace. The better we can use oxygen, the farther and faster we can run.

The benefits of speed work include:

- // maximal development of muscle fiber
- // running economy improvement
- // increased myoglobin
- // improved anaerobic threshold
- // triggering of increased glycogen storage

Another adaptation that occurs through speed work is the increased production of myoglobin. In fact, research tells us that the best way to develop myoglobin is through high-intensity running (above 80 percent VO_2max). Similar to the way hemoglobin carries oxygen to the blood, myoglobin helps transport oxygen to the muscles and then to the mitochondria. With its help, the increased demand for oxygen is met to match capillary delivery and the needs of the mitochondria. Exercise at higher intensities can also increase anaerobic threshold. Basically, the speed intervals provide a two-for-one ticket by developing the anaerobic threshold and VO_2max during the same workout. What's more, because speed sessions include high-intensity running near 100 percent VO_2max (but not over), glycogen stores provide upwards of 90 percent of the energy, thus rapidly depleting them. This, in turn, forces the muscles to adapt and store more glycogen to be used later in workouts.

Speed guidelines

You'll notice that the speed segments in our plans are located toward the beginning of the training block, while later portions are devoted to more half-marathon-specific workouts. This may seem counterintuitive when considering our emphasis on building fitness from the bottom up. However, if speed workouts are executed at the right speeds, it makes sense to include them closer to the beginning of your training cycle. As in other workouts, correct pacing is essential. You will notice that partway through the program, speed work transitions to strength workouts. While runners often worry they will lose the speed gains they have worked so hard to attain, endurance runners (specifically those racing for 90 minutes or more) need not fear. Recall that development of the elements we explain typically occurs at paces above 80 percent of VO_2max. With that said, the speed workouts are shorter intervals ideally at 95–98 percent. The strength workouts are closer to 80 percent but are much longer in duration. We will discuss the strength workouts shortly, but it is important to note that the speed workouts produce the gains, whereas the strength workouts maintain the gains.

When many coaches discuss speed training, they are referring to work that is done at 100 percent VO_2max. In reality, running at 100 percent VO_2max pace can be maintained for only 3–8 minutes. If you are a beginner, 3 minutes is likely more realistic, while an elite miler may be able to continue for close to 8 minutes. Running your speed workouts at or above 100 percent VO_2max, however, causes the structural muscles to begin to break down and forces your system to rely largely on anaerobic sources. This overstresses the anaerobic system and doesn't allow for the positive aerobic adaptations you need to run a good half-marathon. Our program bases speed work on 5K and 10K goal times, races that both last much longer than 3–8 minutes. Rather than working at 100 percent VO_2max, you probably run these distances at 80–95 percent VO_2max. Unlike other plans, the Hansons Method instructs you to complete speed workouts at slightly less than 100 percent VO_2max pace in order to spur maximum physiological adaptations. Go faster, and gains are nullified and injuries are probable.

In addition to pace, the duration of the speed intervals is important. Optimal duration lies between 2 and 8 minutes. If it is too short, the amount of time spent at optimal intensity is minimized, and precious workout time is wasted; if it is too long, lactic acid builds up, and you are too tired to complete the workout at the desired pace. As a result, the length of speed intervals should be adjusted to your ability and experience levels. For example, a 400-meter repeat workout, with each interval lasting around 2 minutes, may be the perfect fit for a beginner. In contrast, the same workout may take an advanced runner 25 percent less time to complete each 400-meter repeat, therefore resulting in fewer benefits.

Recovery is another important part of speed sessions, providing the rest you need to complete another interval. Guidelines for recovery generally state that it should be between 50 and 100 percent of the repeat duration time. For instance, if the repeat is 2 minutes in duration, the recovery should be between 1 and 2 minutes. However, we tend to give beginners longer recovery time at the start of the speed sessions to sustain them throughout the entire workout. We assign recoveries by distance (e.g., 6 × 800 with 400 jog recovery). This usually fits the guidelines for recovery time, especially as the repeat distance increases. With the 12 × 400 meter workout, the recovery time is a little longer. Because it is usually the first speed workout in the segment, we want to ensure it can be completed. Plus it just works better to keep runners moving forward, jogging during the recovery; otherwise there is a tendency to stand around for a few minutes before starting the next repeat.

With further training, recovery can be shortened as an athlete becomes able to handle more work. When doing intervals, one can adjust either the amount of work being done or the amount of recovery allowed. The amount of work is in line with the mileage of the program, however, so we don't want to alter that. But as you become fit, the interval paces may begin to feel easier. In that case, shortening the recovery will provide the same stimulus as earlier in the program. Be aware, however, of running too hard. This session is meant to focus on accumulating time within the desired intensity range, not leave you so tired you can't put in a quality effort. If you run your repeats so hard that you aren't able to jog during your recovery time, you are unlikely to be able to run the next interval at the desired pace. In the end, these speed sessions should total 3 miles of running at that higher intensity, in addition to the warm-up, cooldown, and recovery periods. If you can't get through the intervals to hit 3 miles total, you're running too hard for your abilities and thereby missing out on developing the specific adaptations discussed. That said, if you are a novice runner and completely new to speed workouts, it's better to run only some of the workouts at correct pace than to not run them at all. There's no problem with building up to the scheduled mileage, as needed.

The speed sessions that are utilized throughout the Hansons Half-Marathon Method are provided below. Typically, the schedules start with the lower-duration repeats (10–12 × 400 m) and work up to the longer-duration repeats (4 × 1200 m and 3 × 1600 m). Once the top of the ladder is reached (from the shortest-duration workouts to the longest-duration workouts), you are then free to do the workouts that fit best with your optimal development. Most exercise physiologists agree that this optimal development occurs with intervals that are 2–6 minutes in duration. Anything shorter doesn't stress VO_2max enough, and anything longer tends to stress it too much, creating undue fatigue. So let that be your guide. If the 1600 workout is well above that 6-minute threshold, don't use it. Keep your workouts in that 2–6 minute range per repeat.

For those new to speed work, we strongly encourage joining a local running group. Coaches and more experienced runners can take the guesswork and intimidation out of those first speed workouts by showing you the ropes. When a client tells me he or she has a running group that meets on a certain day during the week, I will do everything I can to schedule that into the training. Additionally, a local track will be your best friend during this phase because it is marked, consistent, and flat. If you are driven by numbers, you can even check your pace every 100 meters to give you nearly constant feedback. This means owning a watch is a must. While your pacing will likely require some trial and error at the beginning, the watch and marked track will help you keep your workouts at the right speeds until pacing becomes second nature.

Here is a chart showing how the speed workouts build on each other. To determine the correct pace for each speed workout, use the pace charts that follow. Find your goal pace for 5K or 10K and run the

SPEED

designated interval as close to that pace as possible. Remember, each session should include a 1- to 3-mile warm-up and cooldown.

SPEED PROGRESSION

WORKOUT	INTERVAL
1	400
2	600
3	800
4	1K
5	1200
6	ladder
7	1600
8	800
9	1600

Note: The Beginner Program has only a 5-week progression of speed.

400 REPEATS PACE CHART

5K GOAL	10K GOAL	400 PACE
15:30	32:30	▶ 1:15
16:00	33:35	▶ 1:18
16:30	34:40	▶ 1:20
17:00	35:45	▶ 1:23
17:30	36:50	▶ 1:25
18:00	37:55	▶ 1:28
18:30	39:00	▶ 1:30
19:00	40:05	▶ 1:33
19:30	41:10	▶ 1:35
20:00	42:15	▶ 1:38
20:30	43:20	▶ 1:40
21:00	44:25	▶ 1:43
21:30	45:30	▶ 1:45
22:00	46:35	▶ 1:48
22:30	47:40	▶ 1:50
23:00	48:45	▶ 1:53
23:30	49:50	▶ 1:55
24:00	50:55	▶ 1:58
24:30	52:00	▶ 2:01
25:00	53:05	▶ 2:03
25:30	54:10	▶ 2:06
26:00	55:15	▶ 2:08
27:00	57:25	▶ 2:13
28:00	59:45	▶ 2:18
29:00	62:05	▶ 2:23
30:00	64:25	▶ 2:28

speed workouts

400 REPEATS

12 × 400 with jog recovery for 50–100% of interval time

Sessions should include a warm-up and cooldown (1–3 mi. each).

600 REPEATS PACE CHART

5K GOAL	10K GOAL	600 PACE
15:30	32:30	▶ 1:52
16:00	33:35	▶ 1:55
16:30	34:40	▶ 1:59
17:00	35:45	▶ 2:03
17:30	36:50	▶ 2:06
18:00	37:55	▶ 2:10
18:30	39:00	▶ 2:14
19:00	40:05	▶ 2:18
19:30	41:10	▶ 2:21
20:00	42:15	▶ 2:25
20:30	43:20	▶ 2:29
21:00	44:25	▶ 2:33
21:30	45:30	▶ 2:36
22:00	46:35	▶ 2:40
22:30	47:40	▶ 2:44
23:00	48:45	▶ 2:48
23:30	49:50	▶ 2:51
24:00	50:55	▶ 2:55
24:30	52:00	▶ 2:59
25:00	53:05	▶ 3:03
25:30	54:10	▶ 3:06
26:00	55:15	▶ 3:10
27:00	57:25	▶ 3:17
28:00	59:45	▶ 3:23
29:00	62:05	▶ 3:30
30:00	64:25	▶ 3:36

speed workouts

600 REPEATS

8 × 600 with jog recovery for 50–100% of interval time

Sessions should include a warm-up and cooldown (1–3 mi. each).

800 REPEATS PACE CHART

5K GOAL	10K GOAL	800 PACE
15:30	32:30	▶ 2:30
16:00	33:35	▶ 2:35
16:30	34:40	▶ 2:40
17:00	35:45	▶ 2:45
17:30	36:50	▶ 2:50
18:00	37:55	▶ 2:55
18:30	39:00	▶ 3:00
19:00	40:05	▶ 3:05
19:30	41:10	▶ 3:10
20:00	42:15	▶ 3:15
20:30	43:20	▶ 3:20
21:00	44:25	▶ 3:25
21:30	45:30	▶ 3:30
22:00	46:35	▶ 3:35
22:30	47:40	▶ 3:40
23:00	48:45	▶ 3:45
23:30	49:50	▶ 3:50
24:00	50:55	▶ 3:55
24:30	52:00	▶ 4:00
25:00	53:05	▶ 4:05
25:30	54:10	▶ 4:10
26:00	55:15	▶ 4:15
27:00	57:25	▶ 4:25
28:00	59:45	▶ 4:35
29:00	62:05	▶ 4:45
30:00	64:25	▶ 4:55

speed workouts

800 REPEATS

6 × 800 with jog recovery for 50–100% of interval time

Sessions should include a warm-up and cooldown (1–3 mi. each).

SPEED

SPEED

1K REPEATS PACE CHART

5K GOAL	10K GOAL	1K PACE
15:30	32:30	▶ 3:06
16:00	33:35	▶ 3:12
16:30	34:40	▶ 3:18
17:00	35:45	▶ 3:24
17:30	36:50	▶ 3:30
18:00	37:55	▶ 3:36
18:30	39:00	▶ 3:42
19:00	40:05	▶ 3:48
19:30	41:10	▶ 3:54
20:00	42:15	▶ 4:00
20:30	43:20	▶ 4:06
21:00	44:25	▶ 4:12
21:30	45:30	▶ 4:18
22:00	46:35	▶ 4:24
22:30	47:40	▶ 4:30
23:00	48:45	▶ 4:36
23:30	49:50	▶ 4:42
24:00	50:55	▶ 4:48
24:30	52:00	▶ 4:54
25:00	53:05	▶ 5:00
25:30	54:10	▶ 5:06
26:00	55:15	▶ 5:12
27:00	57:25	▶ 5:24
28:00	59:45	▶ 5:36
29:00	62:05	▶ 5:48
30:00	64:25	▶ 6:00

speed workouts

1K REPEATS

5 × 1K with jog recovery for 50–100% of interval time

Sessions should include a warm-up and cooldown (1–3 mi. each).

1200 REPEATS PACE CHART

5K GOAL	10K GOAL	1200 PACE
15:30	32:30	▶ 3:42
16:00	33:35	▶ 3:50
16:30	34:40	▶ 3:57
17:00	35:45	▶ 4:05
17:30	36:50	▶ 4:12
18:00	37:55	▶ 4:20
18:30	39:00	▶ 4:27
19:00	40:05	▶ 4:35
19:30	41:10	▶ 4:42
20:00	42:15	▶ 4:50
20:30	43:20	▶ 4:57
21:00	44:25	▶ 5:05
21:30	45:30	▶ 5:12
22:00	46:35	▶ 5:20
22:30	47:40	▶ 5:27
23:00	48:45	▶ 5:35
23:30	49:50	▶ 5:42
24:00	50:55	▶ 5:50
24:30	52:00	▶ 5:57
25:00	53:05	▶ 6:05
25:30	54:10	▶ 6:12
26:00	55:15	▶ 6:20
27:00	57:25	▶ 6:36
28:00	59:45	▶ 6:51
29:00	62:05	▶ 7:07
30:00	64:25	▶ 7:23

SPEED

speed workouts

1200 REPEATS

4 × 1200 with jog recovery for 50–100% of interval time

Sessions should include a warm-up and cooldown (1–3 mi. each).

$$\frac{6:20}{1.2} = \frac{x}{1}$$

5.2 min/km
8.32 min/miler

5.2 min = min
1.?

ladder PACE CHART

5K GOAL	10K GOAL	400 PACE	800 PACE	1200 PACE	1600 PACE
15:30	32:30	1:15	2:30	3:42	5:00
16:00	33:35	1:18	2:35	3:50	5:10
16:30	34:40	1:20	2:40	3:57	5:20
17:00	35:45	1:23	2:45	4:05	5:30
17:30	36:50	1:25	2:50	4:12	5:40
18:00	37:55	1:28	2:54	4:20	5:50
18:30	39:00	1:30	2:59	4:27	6:00
19:00	40:05	1:33	3:04	4:35	6:10
19:30	41:10	1:35	3:09	4:42	6:20
20:00	42:15	1:38	3:14	4:50	6:30
20:30	43:20	1:40	3:19	4:57	6:40
21:00	44:25	1:43	3:24	5:05	6:50
21:30	45:30	1:45	3:29	5:12	7:00
22:00	46:35	1:48	3:34	5:20	7:10
22:30	47:40	1:50	3:39	5:27	7:20
23:00	48:45	1:53	3:44	5:35	7:30
23:30	49:50	1:55	3:49	5:42	7:40
24:00	50:55	1:58	3:54	5:50	7:50
24:30	52:00	2:01	3:59	5:57	8:00
25:00	53:05	2:03	4:04	6:05	8:10
25:30	54:10	2:06	4:09	6:12	8:20
26:00	55:15	2:08	4:14	6:20	8:30
27:00	57:25	2:13	4:25	6:36	8:50
28:00	59:45	2:18	4:35	6:51	9:10
29:00	62:05	2:23	4:45	7:07	9:30
30:00	64:25	2:28	4:55	7:23	9:50

SPEED

speed workouts

LADDER

400-800-1200-1600-1200-800-400 with jog recovery for 50–100% of interval time

Sessions should include a warm-up and cooldown (1–3 mi. each).

1600 REPEATS PACE CHART

5K GOAL	10K GOAL	1600 PACE
15:30	32:30	▶ 5:00
16:00	33:35	▶ 5:10
16:30	34:40	▶ 5:20
17:00	35:45	▶ 5:30
17:30	36:50	▶ 5:40
18:00	37:55	▶ 5:50
18:30	39:00	▶ 6:00
19:00	40:05	▶ 6:10
19:30	41:10	▶ 6:20
20:00	42:15	▶ 6:30
20:30	43:20	▶ 6:40
21:00	44:25	▶ 6:50
21:30	45:30	▶ 7:00
22:00	46:35	▶ 7:10
22:30	47:40	▶ 7:20
23:00	48:45	▶ 7:30
23:30	49:50	▶ 7:40
24:00	50:55	▶ 7:50
24:30	52:00	▶ 8:00
25:00	53:05	▶ 8:10
25:30	54:10	▶ 8:20
26:00	55:15	▶ 8:30
27:00	57:25	▶ 8:50
28:00	59:45	▶ 9:10
29:00	62:05	▶ 9:30
30:00	64:25	▶ 9:50

SPEED

speed workouts

1600 REPEATS

3 × 1600 with jog recovery for 50–100% of interval time

Sessions should include a warm-up and cooldown (1–3 mi. each).

STRENGTH WORKOUTS

After spending a number of weeks performing periodic speed sessions, the muscle fibers and physiological systems will have adapted and will be ready for more endurance-specific adaptations. When strength workouts are added to the schedule, the goal of training shifts from improving the VO_2max (along with anaerobic threshold) to maintaining the VO_2max and preparing the body to handle the fatigue associated with endurance running. You'll notice that at the same time the strength segment begins, the tempo runs and the long runs become more substantial. At this point in the plan, everything the runner is doing is focused solely on half-marathon preparation.

When we talk about strength workouts, we aren't referring to intense sessions in the weight room, pumping iron and flexing muscles. Strength workouts are still runs, but ones that emphasize volume at a slightly lower intensity, with the goal of stressing the aerobic system at a high level. While the speed sessions are designed to be short enough to avoid lactate accumulation (even though intensity is very high), the strength sessions are meant to force the runner to adapt to running longer distances with moderate amounts of lactate accumulation.

Physiology of strength workouts

Over time, strength sessions improve anaerobic capacities, meaning you will be able to tolerate higher levels of lactic acid and produce less of it at higher intensities. While your body may have shut down in response to the lactic acid buildup at the beginning of training, strength sessions help to train your muscles to work through the discomfort of lactic acid accumulation. Additionally, these workouts teach your exercising muscles to get better at removing lactic acid, as well as improving your running economy and allowing you to use less oxygen at the same effort. Strength workouts also spur development of something called fractional utilization of maximal capacity. In practical terms, this development allows a person to run at a faster pace for a longer time, which leads to an increase in anaerobic threshold. For the half-marathon, this means conserving glycogen for those running more than 90 minutes for the race. For faster runners, it means being able to tolerate moderate amounts of lactic acid and higher-intensity running for longer amounts of time.

The benefits of strength workouts include:

// improved lactate clearance

// improved lactate tolerance

// improved endurance at faster paces

// improved oxygen delivery (via stronger heart)

// improved running economy

These adaptations all begin with an increase in the size of the heart's ventricle chamber. During a strength workout, the heart is required to pump faster and with more force than during easier runs. It is not being worked quite as hard as during a speed session, but it works at a fairly high intensity for significantly longer. The end result is a stronger heart muscle with a larger chamber area, which means an increased stroke volume. (The stroke volume is the amount of blood pumped from the left ventricle per beat.) This results in more blood being sent to the exercising muscles, hence delivering more oxygen. In addition, strength workouts help to involve the intermediate muscle fibers, increasing their oxidative capacities. Within the muscles, less lactate ends up being produced at faster speeds, and the lactate that is produced is recycled back into usable fuel. For practical reasons, strength workouts are important because running at faster paces, especially near anaerobic threshold, begins to feel easier, economy is improved, and stamina is increased. As you can see, the benefits of strength workouts are practically boundless.

Strength guidelines

For most runners, the strength repeats will fall somewhere between 60 and 80 percent of VO_2max, which will be slower than the speed sessions. You can stretch that out to 85–90 percent of VO_2max for faster runners. However, while the speed sessions are relatively short (e.g., 3 × 1600 m) with moderate recovery, the strength sessions are double the volume (e.g., 6 miles of higher-intensity running) with much shorter relative recovery. Strength workouts are designed to be run 10 seconds per mile faster than goal race pace. If your goal half-marathon pace is 8:00 minutes per mile, then your strength pace will be 7:50 per mile. The faster the runner, the closer this corresponds to 10K pace, but for the novice, it is between goal half-marathon pace and 10K pace, probably pretty close to 15K pace. Your pace is indicated in Table 3.5. Faster runners will already be near that 10-second number, and novice runners will likely be at a slightly slower pace. While you practice half-marathon pace with the tempo runs, the strength workouts are faster to get your body accustomed to the stress of lactic acid buildup, stressing the anaerobic threshold, which happens to coincide with the 10-second-faster pace (or half-marathon pace). This faster overall time will bring along with it a large increase in lactic acid. Even though the strength workout may not feel hard from an intensity standpoint, the volume, coupled with short recovery periods, is enough to stimulate lactic acid accumulation and make way for positive adaptations. Refer to Table 3.4 for a quick guide to strength sessions.

TABLE **3.4** STRENGTH SESSION QUICK GUIDE	
SESSION	**GOAL**
strength pace	10 sec./mi. faster than marathon goal pace
strength recovery	short relative to repeat duration
repeat volume	1–3 mi. per repeat
total strength volume	6 mi. at strength pace

As mentioned earlier, recovery is key to the success of these strength sessions. To maintain a certain level of lactic acid, the recovery is kept to a fraction of the repeat duration. For instance, the 6 × 1-mile strength workout calls for a recovery jog of a quarter mile between each interval. If the repeats are to be done at 8:00-minute pace, the quarter-mile jog will end up being between 2:30 and 3:00 minutes of jogging, totaling less than 50 percent of the duration of the intervals. Because these are less intense intervals than the speed intervals, you may be tempted to exceed the prescribed pace, but keep in mind that the adaptations you're looking for specifically occur at that speed, no faster.

These strength workouts cover a lot of ground, so try to locate a marked bike path or loop on which to execute them. While a track can be used, the workouts get monotonous and injury is more likely, due to the increased torque on the lower legs from turning so often. Remember to always add 1.5 to 3 miles for a warm-up and a cooldown.

Begin with 1 mile and progress each week to the next longer distance. Once all workouts have been completed, proceed back down the distances. Basically, you will begin with 1-mile intervals, progress to 3-mile intervals, then work back down to 1-mile intervals. To determine the correct pace for each strength workout, use the pace charts that follow. Find your goal half-marathon pace and run the designated interval as close to that pace as possible.

STRENGTH PROGRESSION

WORKOUT	INTERVAL
1	1 mi.
2	1.5 mi.
3	2 mi.
4	3 mi.
5	2 mi.
6	1.5 mi.
7	1 mi.

1-mile REPEATS PACE CHART

HALF-MARATHON GOAL	MILE PACE
1:02:30	4:36
1:04:45	4:46
1:01:07	4:57
1:09:30	5:08
1:12:00	5:20
1:14:00	6:29
1:17:00	5:42
1:19:00	5:52
1:21:30	6:01
1:24:00	6:14
1:26:00	6:24
1:29:00	6:37
1:31:00	6:46
1:33:30	6:58
1:36:00	7:09
1:38:00	7:19
1:41:00	7:32
1:43:00	7:41
1:45:00	7:51
1:48:00	8:04
1:50:00	8:13
1:53:00	8:27
1:55:00	8:36
2:02:00	9:08
2:10:00	9:45
2:17:00	10:17
2:24:00	10:49

strength workouts

1-MILE REPEATS

3 × 1 miles with 800 jog recovery

Sessions should include a warm-up and cooldown (1–3 mi. each).

STRENGTH

1.5-mile REPEATS PACE CHART

HALF-MARATHON GOAL	1.5-MILE PACE
1:02:30	▶ 6:54
1:04:45	▶ 7:09
1:01:07	▶ 7:25
1:09:30	▶ 7:42
1:12:00	▶ 8:00
1:14:00	▶ 8:13
1:17:00	▶ 8:33
1:19:00	▶ 8:48
1:21:30	▶ 9:01
1:24:00	▶ 9:21
1:26:00	▶ 9:36
1:29:00	▶ 9:55
1:31:00	▶ 10:09
1:33:30	▶ 10:27
1:36:00	▶ 10:43
1:38:00	▶ 10:58
1:41:00	▶ 11:18
1:43:00	▶ 11:31
1:45:00	▶ 11:46
1:48:00	▶ 12:06
1:50:00	▶ 12:19
1:53:00	▶ 12:40
1:55:00	▶ 12:54
2:02:00	▶ 13:42
2:10:00	▶ 14:37
2:17:00	▶ 15:25
2:24:00	▶ 16:13

STRENGTH

strength workouts

1.5-MILE REPEATS

4 × 1.5 miles with 800 jog recovery

Sessions should include a warm-up and cooldown (1–3 mi. each).

2-mile REPEATS PACE CHART

HALF-MARATHON GOAL	2-MILE PACE
1:02:30	▶ 9:12
1:04:45	▶ 9:32
1:01:07	▶ 9:54
1:09:30	▶ 10:16
1:12:00	▶ 10:40
1:14:00	▶ 10:58
1:17:00	▶ 11:24
1:19:00	▶ 11:44
1:21:30	▶ 12:02
1:24:00	▶ 12:28
1:26:00	▶ 12:48
1:29:00	▶ 13:14
1:31:00	▶ 13:32
1:33:30	▶ 13:56
1:36:00	▶ 14:18
1:38:00	▶ 14:38
1:41:00	▶ 15:04
1:43:00	▶ 15:22
1:45:00	▶ 15:42
1:48:00	▶ 16:08
1:50:00	▶ 16:26
1:53:00	▶ 16:54
1:55:00	▶ 17:12
2:02:00	▶ 18:16
2:10:00	▶ 19:30
2:17:00	▶ 20:34
2:24:00	▶ 21:38

strength workouts

2-MILE REPEATS

3 × 2 miles with 800 jog recovery

Sessions should include a warm-up and cooldown (1–3 mi. each).

STRENGTH

3-mile REPEATS PACE CHART

HALF-MARATHON GOAL	3-MILE PACE
1:02:30	13:48
1:04:45	14:18
1:01:07	14:51
1:09:30	15:24
1:12:00	16:00
1:14:00	16:27
1:17:00	17:06
1:19:00	17:36
1:21:30	18:03
1:24:00	18:42
1:26:00	19:12
1:29:00	19:51
1:31:00	20:18
1:33:30	20:54
1:36:00	21:27
1:38:00	21:57
1:41:00	22:36
1:43:00	23:03
1:45:00	23:33
1:48:00	24:12
1:50:00	24:39
1:53:00	25:21
1:55:00	25:48
2:02:00	27:24
2:10:00	29:55
2:17:00	30:51
2:24:00	32:27

strength workouts

3-MILE REPEATS

2 × 3 miles with 800 jog recovery

Sessions should include a warm-up and cooldown (1–3 mi. each).

STRENGTH

TEMPO WORKOUTS

Tempo runs have long been a staple of all good endurance training plans, so most experienced runners have encountered them before. Tempo runs have been defined in numerous ways, but in the Hansons Half-Marathon Method, they are defined as race pace runs. Over the course of training, your tempo runs will span a number of months, requiring you to maintain race pace through an assortment of challenges and circumstances.

Internalizing pace is one of the most difficult training components for runners to master. If you feel great at the start line and go out 30 seconds per mile faster than you planned, you'll likely hit the halfway point ready to throw in the towel. No significant half-marathon records have ever been set via a positive split (running the second half of the race slower than the first half). In fact, nearly every world record, regardless of distance, has been set using negative or even splits. The good news is that half-marathon tempo training runs are quite fast, making them harder to mistakenly hammer than, say, the relatively slower marathon tempo runs. However, remember this: If you want to have a successful half-marathon performance, you are better off maintaining a steady pace throughout the entire race rather than following the "fly and die" method. Tempo runs teach you an important skill: control. Even when the pace feels easy, these runs train you to hold back and maintain. Additionally, tempo runs provide a great staging ground for experimenting with different fluids, gels, and other nutritionals. Because tempo runs have you running at your intended half-marathon pace, you get a very good idea of what your body can and cannot handle. The same goes for your gear. Use the tempo runs as dress rehearsals to try various shoes and outfits to determine what is most comfortable. Regardless of training, these details can make or break your race; tempo runs provide perfect opportunities to fine-tune your race day plans.

Physiology of tempo workouts

In the same way that easy and long runs improve endurance, so do tempo runs. Specifically, tempo runs improve race-specific endurance. Although they are faster than easy runs, they are well under anaerobic threshold and thus provide many of the same adaptations. Too, the benefits of longer tempo runs mimic those of long runs, since the aerobic system is worked in similar ways. Specifically, from a physiological standpoint, the tempo run has a great positive impact on running economy at your goal race pace. One of the most visible benefits of this is increased endurance throughout a long race. Indeed, as during the long run, the ability to burn fat is highly specified during tempo runs. The run is just fast enough that the aerobic system is challenged to keep up with a high percentage of fat oxidation, but it's slow enough that the mitochondria and supporting fibers can barely keep up.

The benefits of tempo work include:

// helps you to internalize half-marathon goal pace
// teaches you to control and maintain pace
// chance to experiment with nutrition, hydration, gear
// improved running economy at goal pace
// improved endurance

Over time, it is the tempo run that will indicate whether or not you have selected the right half-marathon goal. We have always considered this workout more telling than any other. Because the tempo run offers no break between intervals or rest periods, if you continually struggle to hit the correct pace for long tempo runs, there will be some question as to whether you can hold that pace for an entire race.

The greatest benefit that these workouts offer is the opportunity to firmly learn your desired race pace through repetition. With time, your body figures out a way to internalize how that pace feels, eventually making it second nature. When runners cannot tell if they are close to pace, the tendency is to be off pace (usually too fast), setting them up for unavoidable doom. Learning your pace and knowing how it feels can make the difference between a good race and a bad race.

Tempo workout guidelines

In the Hansons Half-Marathon Method, the tempo run is completed at goal race pace. For many other coaches, a tempo run is much shorter, at paces closer to strength pace, but for our purposes, tempo and half-marathon paces are interchangeable. You should run at goal pace, even early on when it may feel easy. It will take a good number of tempo workouts before you fully internalize the pace and can regulate your runs based on feel. What does change throughout training is the distance of these workouts. Tempo runs are progressively longer, with an adjustment every few weeks; they increase from 3 miles for a beginner and 5 miles for an advanced runner to 7 miles over the last few weeks of training. As an advanced runner begins to reach the heaviest mileage, the total volume of a tempo run, along with a warm-up and a cooldown, can reach 12–14 miles and approach 90 minutes in length.

With the long run looming after a tempo run, that 12-miler might look a lot tougher than it did initially. Remember the principle of cumulative fatigue? This is a prime example of how the Hansons Method employs it. Suddenly that fairly easy longer run mimics the fatigue you will feel during the later portion of the half-marathon. Rather than sending you into the long run feeling fresh, we try to simulate those last miles of the half-marathon, and there's nothing like a tempo run to put a little fatigue in your legs.

TEMPO PROGRESSION FOR BEGINNER RUNNERS

WEEKS	DISTANCE
5	easy mileage
3	3 mi.
3	5 mi.
3	6 mi.
3	7 mi.

TEMPO PROGRESSION FOR ADVANCED RUNNERS

WEEKS	DISTANCE
2	easy mileage
3	3 mi.
3	4 mi.
3	5 mi.
3	6 mi.
3	7 mi.

tempo PACE CHART

HALF-MARATHON GOAL	MILE PACE
2:24:00	10:59
2:17:00	10:27
2:10:00	9:55
2:02:00	9:18
1:55:00	8:46
1:53:00	8:37
1:50:00	8:23
1:48:00	8:14
1:45:00	8:01
1:43:00	7:51
1:41:00	7:42
1:38:00	7:29
1:36:00	7:19
1:33:30	7:08
1:31:00	6:56
1:29:00	6:47
1:26:00	6:34
1:24:00	6:24
1:21:30	6:13
1:19:00	6:02
1:17:00	5:52
1:14:00	5:39
1:12:00	5:30
1:09:30	5:18
1:07:00	5:07
1:04:45	4:56
1:02:30	4:46

tempo workout

5-10 MILES

Sessions should include a warm-up and cooldown (1–3 mi. each).

TEMPO

How to pace workouts

To help you further understand the intensity at which you should be running during the various workouts in the training plan, check out Figure 3.3. The diagonal line represents a sample VO_2max of a runner. The first line on the left is for the easy running days and represents everything under the aerobic threshold; it is the largest but also the slowest area. The next line is the long run and represents the fastest paces a person should run for the long run, but it could also represent the fastest of easy days for beginners. The middle line denotes ideal tempo pace and, therefore, half-marathon goal pace. It is above aerobic threshold but below anaerobic threshold. The strength line represents the high end of the "lactate" section, as strength runs should fall just below anaerobic threshold. Finally, there is the speed line, which represents where speed workouts should fall, which is just below VO_2max.

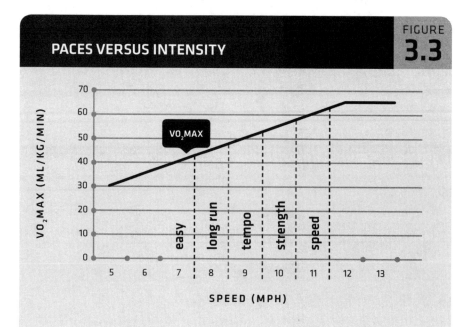

PACES VERSUS INTENSITY

FIGURE
3.3

As VO$_2$max and running speed increase, thresholds and zones can be indicated.

1. Easy pace zone
2. Moderate pace zone
3. Marathon pace zone
4. Tempo pace zone (half-marathon pace)
5. Strength pace zone (10–15K pace)
6. Speed pace zone (5–10K pace)

With this continuum in mind, it becomes clear why running faster than you're instructed to run compromises development. Not only do you miss out on the benefits the workout was meant to provide when you go too fast, but you also increase fatigue. The essential point is this: Paces are there for a specific reason. While some runners feel that paces hold them back, in reality proper pacing will propel you forward in the end. Fight the temptation to buy into the "If some is good, more is better" mentality, and keep in mind the specific goal of each particular workout.

The taper

While it may seem counterintuitive at best and like a waste of time at worst, believe me when I say that cutting mileage and intensity is an integral part of half-marathon training when done at the right times. When you reach the final stretch of training, your goal is to recover from all that work you have put in, while also maintaining the improvements you made over the past few months. Reducing your training at this point, called tapering, is one of the keys to successful racing.

The mistake many runners make with their taper is that they cut everything, including mileage, workouts, intensity, and easy days. In the same way we instruct you not to add these components too soon, we also suggest not abruptly cutting them out. When runners subtract too much training too quickly, they often feel sluggish and even more fatigued than they did when they were in their peak training days. By cutting the training back gradually, you'll feel fresh and ready to race.

An SOS workout takes about 10 days to demonstrate the physiological improvement. That's right, it takes more than a week before you reap any benefits from a hard run. Just as important to consider, the immediate effect of a hard workout is fatigue. So if you try to do something after a hard effort, you are just digging yourself a hole. Yet, if you wait too long, the benefits have come and gone. If you look at the training plans in the Hansons Method, you'll notice that the last SOS workout is done 10 days prior to the half-marathon because after that point, SOS workouts will do nothing but make you tired for the big day. We also implement roughly a 50–55 percent reduction in overall volume (depending on which schedule you are following) during the last 7 days of the program. Despite this, you will still run the same number of days per week, with only the daily mileage reduced. For a parallel, consider how you would feel if you were accustomed to drinking a couple of cups of coffee in the morning and then suddenly gave it up cold turkey. Your body probably would react with a dull headache. If instead you cut back to one cup, you limit the effects of withdrawal and usually end up feeling better. This is the same idea—reduce the stress while keeping the body happy and in its preestablished routine. By continuing to run fewer miles, but still running the same number of days, you reduce the number of variables that are adjusted. Instead of reducing frequency, volume, and intensity, you are tinkering only with the last two. The problem with many training plans is that they cut too much out of the schedule and prescribe a lengthy taper, causing a runner to lose some of those hard-earned fitness gains. By subscribing to a 10-day gentle taper period, you cut down on the risk of losing any of those gains but still allow adequate time for rest and recovery.

From a physiological standpoint, the taper fits well with the principle of cumulative fatigue because the training program does not allow you to completely recover until you reach those final 10 days. Over the last couple of months of the program, some of the good hormones, enzymes, and functions in your body have been suppressed through incomplete recovery, while the by-products of fatigue have simultaneously been building. With reduced intensity and volume during the taper, these good functions flourish. Meanwhile, the by-products are allowed to completely break down, and the body is left in a state of readiness for your best performance. We always warn runners not to underestimate the power of the taper. If you are worried about your ability to run a complete half-marathon at the pace of your tempo runs, consider this: The taper can elicit improvements of up to 3 percent. That is the difference between a 2:00 half-marathon and a 1:58 half-marathon. It is a bit like getting something for nothing. And at this stage of my career, a nearly 2-minute improvement in my half-marathon best would be amazing.

Training intensity chart

To be utilized in determining how fast to run your workouts, Table 3.5 demonstrates pace per mile based on various goal half-marathon times. For easy runs, refer to the easy aerobic A and easy aerobic B columns. The faster end of the long run spectrum is indicated in the moderate aerobic column. The marathon column is useful for those who have marathon experience and are looking to come back down to the half-marathon. It's really more for comparison purposes than anything. The half-marathon pace is the speed at which your tempo runs

PACE CHART FOR VARIOUS TRAINING INTENSITIES*

MARATHON GOAL	HALF-MARATHON GOAL	RECOVERY	AEROBIC A/EASY	AEROBIC B/EASY
5:00:00	2:24:00	14:22	13:32	12:41
4:45:00	2:17:00	13:43	12:55	12:05
4:30:00	2:10:00	13:02	12:16	11:28
4:15:00	2:02:00	12:22	11:38	10:52
4:00:00	· 1:55:00	11:42	11:00	10:15
3:55:00	1:53:00	11:28	10:40	10:00
3:50:00	1:50:00	11:15	10:34	9:51
3:45:00	1:48:00	11:01	10:21	9:39
3:40:00	1:45:00	10:48	10:08	9:27
3:35:00	1:43:00	10:34	9:55	9:14
3:30:00	1:41:00	10:19	9:41	9:02
3:25:00	1:38:00	10:06	9:28	8:49
3:20:00	1:36:00	9:53	9:16	8:38
3:15:00	1:33:30	9:38	9:02	8:25
3:10:00	1:31:00	9:25	8:49	8:13
3:05:00	1:29:00	9:11	8:36	8:01
3:00:00	1:26:00	8:57	8:23	7:48
2:55:00	1:24:00	8:43	8:10	7:36
2:50:00	1:21:30	8:28	7:56	7:23
2:45:00	1:19:00	8:15	7:43	7:11
2:40:00	1:17:00	8:00	7:30	6:58
2:35:00	1:14:00	7:46	7:17	6:46
2:30:00	1:12:00	7:32	7:03	6:34
2:25:00	1:09:30	7:18	6:50	6:21
2:20:00	1:07:00	7:03	6:36	6:08
2:15:00	1:04:45	6:49	6:23	5:56
2:10:00	1:02:30	6:35	6:09	5:43

*All paces are per mile.

MODERATE AEROBIC/ LONG RUN	MARATHON PACE/ TEMPO	STRENGTH	10K SPEED	5K SPEED
12:16	11:27	11:17	10:30	10:04
11:41	10:52	10:42	9:58	9:34
11:05	10:18	10:08	9:27	9:04
10:29	9:44	9:34	8:55	8:33
9:53	9:09	8:59	8:24	8:03
9:38	8:58	8:48	8:13	7:53
9:29	8:46	8:36	8:03	7:43
9:18	8:35	8:25	7:52	7:33
9:06	8:23	8:13	7:42	7:23
8:53	8:12	8:02	7:31	7:13
8:42	8:01	7:51	7:21	7:03
8:29	7:49	7:39	7:10	6:53
8:18	7:38	7:28	7:00	6:43
8:05	7:26	7:16	6:49	6:33
7:54	7:15	7:05	6:39	6:23
7:42	7:03	6:53	6:28	6:12
7:29	6:52	6:42	6:18	6:02
7:17	6:40	6:30	6:07	5:52
7:05	6:29	6:19	5:57	5:42
6:53	6:18	6:08	5:46	5:32
6:41	6:06	5:56	5:36	5:22
6:29	5:55	5:45	5:25	5:12
6:17	5:43	5:33	5:15	5:02
6:05	5:32	5:22	5:04	4:52
5:52	5:20	5:10	4:54	4:42
5:40	5:09	4:59	4:43	4:32
5:28	4:57	4:47	4:33	4:22

should be run. The strength column will be your reference for strength workouts, and the 10K and 5K columns for your speed workouts. Keep in mind that actual 5K and 10K race times will be more accurate than this chart. If you have raced those distances, use your finishing times to guide your speed workouts. Our goal here is to provide you with some guidance for your workouts, keeping you focused and making the correct physiological adaptations throughout training.

4

Hansons
training plans

WHEN I THINK OF the half-marathon, I don't think of half the distance of a marathon, or half the work needed to complete it. Rather, the half distance has a strong identity of its own, one that demands respect and a serious commitment to training. In a way, the half-marathon is like the melting pot of the running world or like a bridge across the gap between the 10K race distance and the full marathon. For runners who have already been through the marathon journey, it's a road going back to a perhaps forgotten time of faster training. This can present a challenge. For those who haven't ventured to the marathon distance yet but would like to, the half is a landing zone that makes that faraway goal of a marathon seem more attainable.

When Keith and Kevin set out to create the Hansons Method of training for long-distance races, they did so with average runners in mind, hoping to give them an alternative to the status quo programs already in existence. Since that time, thousands of runners have used our programs and found great success, a testament not only to Kevin and Keith's coaching know-how but also to the programs themselves.

In this chapter you will find not only our Beginner Program and Advanced Program but also our Just Finish Program. Read through these descriptions to decide which program is the best fit for your experience and ability levels. Miles logged, training history, ambition, and race experience are all key factors in deciding which level will suit you best. Whichever program you choose, if you follow it faithfully, you can expect to reach your half-marathon goal.

HALF-MARATHON PROGRAM	TYPE OF RUNNER
Just Finish	simply wants to complete the race, no specific time goal
Beginner	new to half-marathon distance, has raced shorter distances, lower mileage base
Advanced	experienced half-marathon runner, competitive racer, higher mileage base

One important caveat for those choosing the Beginner or Advanced Program: If you have never run a race of any distance, or even trained consistently, such as running at least 10–15 miles per week for at least 3 straight weeks, you should first evaluate your readiness to begin one of the two plans. Bypassing shorter races such as 5Ks and 10Ks is not recommended. We suggest that true novices first dedicate a bit of training to shorter races, as well as up their base miles, before jumping into these half-marathon programs. While the Beginner Program has some base miles built into the beginning, it will only help you if you come into training with some kind of base of your own. What we offer here will get you to your goals, but make no mistake: The programs are not easy. And without a proper buildup of mileage, you will set yourself up for potential injury or overtraining. The exception here is the Just Finish Program, which I will discuss in more detail later in this chapter.

The Beginner Program

The Beginner Program takes the runner from 10 miles per week and builds to the upper 40s during peak weeks. Although we name this the Beginner Program, it is not designed for the absolute running newbie. It works well for someone who is new to half-marathoning but has some experience and mileage under his or her belt, such as a runner who has run mileage in the 30 mile per week range and run a variety of 5K and 10K races but never a half. We also recommend this plan to experienced runners who have previously tackled the 13.1-mile distance but done so with a minimal-type training program. Not uncommonly, some runners have run a half-marathon before but have done so using a program aimed at simply finishing, and they have trained by doing the smallest amount possible. For them, the Beginner Program (Table 4.1) may be more advanced than what they trained with previously, making it the appropriate next progression in their training.

Finally, if you haven't run higher mileage before, this program may be a good fit.

The initial 4 weeks of the Beginner Program are designed to simply build your weekly mileage. It's all about time on your feet and miles logged. The best way to bank mileage safely is to reduce intensity (no SOS workouts) and spread a moderate amount of mileage over a number of days. It is during these first 4 weeks that the body adapts to the stress of regular training, preparing it for the next phase.

For runners coming to the Beginner Program who are already logging weekly mileage closer to that specified in the 3rd or 4th week of training, just keep doing what you are doing and let the training catch up with you.

Following the 4-week base phase, we begin to turn up the heat or, rather, the intensity. You will notice two new additions: speed and tempo. The speed workouts are executed at 5K or 10K pace (refer to Chapter 3 for specific workouts). These workouts include 12 × 400 repeats, 8 × 600 repeats, 6 × 800 repeats, and beyond. We throw different types of workouts at you both to keep things interesting and to achieve the desired physiological adaptations. While you will only run a total of 3 miles at these faster paces, the total mileage for the day will be greater once you add in the recovery intervals and a warm-up and a cooldown. Runners using the Beginner Program should warm up and cool down for 1–2 miles (which adds 2–4 miles to your workout). This remains one of the most important parts of training throughout the program because warming up and cooling down help to boost performance and speed up the recovery process following workouts.

Some will question why the speed-oriented training block is scheduled prior to other phases, such as strength. In addition to the important physiological adaptations that occur as a result of speed training, it gives a beginner an excellent opportunity to establish a baseline. If you don't have any idea what pace you should be shooting for in the half-marathon, complete several speed workouts, and you will soon find out. For runners who have never run a 5K (or haven't done so in the recent past), much less a half-marathon, we encourage you to sign up for a 5K or 10K race. Optimally, adjust your training plan slightly so that you get a race in during the 8th week of your plan, 3 weeks into your speed work (see Table 5.1). This will help you determine an appropriate training goal for the half-marathon-specific training block that is approaching in coming weeks.

Speed workouts also make great dress rehearsals for the strength sessions. They allow you to make mistakes and learn lessons about pacing and recovery early on before starting those important half-marathon-specific workouts. Finally, speed workouts help a runner develop supreme mental toughness. For those who are accustomed to lacing up their shoes and heading out the door for the same low-key 30- to 60-minute jog each day, speed workouts provide a new challenge, for both the mind and the body. These sessions force you to run at a higher intensity for a longer time, drawing you out of your comfort zone and into new territory. Remember, the only way to improve fitness is by bumping it up from the bottom; each time you step slightly out of your comfort zone, your body responds to the new stimulus. When you learn to tolerate discomfort for longer and longer durations, the payoff is multifold: You gain speed, discover your true potential, and become comfortable with higher-intensity training. What's more, you also develop a higher anaerobic threshold and aerobic capacity without ever training beyond VO_2max and risking injury.

Around the time we add speed to the training schedule, tempo workouts also come into play. Assisting in self-regulation and pacing, tempo runs are to be completed at goal half-marathon pace. Just as before and after speed workouts, you should complete a 1- to 2-mile warm-up and cooldown with tempo runs. Thus, in the end, although a tempo run itself may be 5 miles, the total mileage will be closer to 7–9 miles. As the tempo distance increases, these workouts total somewhere in the neighborhood of 8–11 miles, 6–7 of which are at goal half-marathon pace. You may be surprised by the ease with which you complete the first few tempo runs, since they are fairly short. As they get longer, however, you probably will find it tougher to sustain that half-marathon pace. Just remind yourself that this is excellent practice and is getting you ready for race day!

Once you have begun to master speed and tempo, you approach the more half-marathon-specific training. At this point in the program, the speed workouts give way to strength workouts, and the tempo runs become much longer. The long runs also peak in mileage, and the weekly volume is at its highest. We won't sugarcoat this phase; it is difficult, and you will be tired. You'll find that strength workouts are similar in structure to speed sessions, with the main differences being in volume and pace. While speed workouts totaled around 3 miles with the speed at a 5–10K pace, strength workouts hit 6 miles and are completed at goal half-marathon pace minus 10 seconds per mile. For instance, if your goal half-marathon pace is 10:00 minutes per mile, your strength workout pace will be 9:50 per mile. For specific speed and strength workouts, refer to Chapter 3.

As we alluded, this final section of SOS training is meant to be difficult and leave you feeling somewhat drained. That being said, you've adhered to the principle of cumulative fatigue all along, so your body will be accustomed to handling new challenges on tired legs. Of course you want to avoid entering this section overtrained. If you ran the previous blocks too hard, you won't have any fuel in the tank to tackle strength sessions. Through this section of training, the improvements will come from the higher weekly volume, which is why it is particularly important to stick to the paces we advise. Running too fast during high-mileage weeks is sure to leave you injured or burned-out.

You'll notice that the long runs are placed consistently throughout the program, although they get longer as you get further into training. It is this aspect of the program, the long run, that sparks the most questions, in particular about their progression and frequency. Following several weeks of shorter easy runs, we begin with a 10-mile Sunday long run, increasing that run by no more than 2 miles from one week to the next. These increases are proportionate to the scheduled weekly mileage, meaning the long run makes up about 25 percent of the weekly mileage throughout the program. As the tempo runs begin to increase, so too do the long runs. For instance, during a week with a 10- to 12-mile long run, there is also a tempo run of 5–6 miles, but with warm-up and cooldown, that day will also total close to 10 miles. The reason we have a long run one week and a regular training run the next week is to accommodate those longer tempo runs. Without this adjustment, you'd essentially end up doing three long runs every 8 days for more than a month, throwing off the balance of training and increasing your risk of injury. By doing a more traditional higher-mileage long run every 2 weeks, your body learns to handle the larger volume while still running at least one run per week of significant volume.

The icing on the half-marathon training cake is the easiest section of the program: the taper. After all that hard training, the body is fatigued. There may have been moments when you wondered if you'd even complete the training. The purpose of this last block is to finally let the body recover from the previous 16 weeks, all while maintaining the fitness that was gained. We don't want you feeling fresh during the majority of training, but the opposite is true during these last 10 days before the big race. This is your time to get a little rest but also to hold on to all those positive adaptations your body has made up to this point.

TABLE 4.1	HANSONS HALF-MARATHON METHOD: BEGINNER PROGRAM

WEEK	MON	TUES	WED	THURS
1			OFF	easy 3 mi.
2	OFF	easy 2 mi.	OFF	easy 3 mi.
3	OFF	easy 4 mi.	OFF	easy 4 mi.
4	OFF	easy 5 mi.	OFF	easy 3 mi.
5	OFF	easy 5 mi.	OFF	3 mi.
6	easy 4 mi.	12 × 400	OFF	3 mi.
7	easy 4 mi.	8 × 600	OFF	3 mi.
8	easy 6 mi.	6 × 800	OFF	4 mi.
9	easy 5 mi.	5 × 1K	OFF	4 mi.
10	easy 6 mi.	4 × 1200	OFF	4 mi.

SPEED (Tues, weeks 6–10) · TEMPO (Thurs, weeks 5–10)

SPEED WORKOUTS
See pace charts, pp. 73–79

STRENGTH WORKOUTS
See pace charts, pp. 85–88

TEMPO WORKOUTS
See pace chart, p. 93

BEGINNER

FRI	SAT	SUN	WEEKLY TOTAL	WEEK
OFF	easy 3 mi.	easy 4 mi.	▶ **10** MI.	1
easy 3 mi.	easy 3 mi.	easy 4 mi.	▶ **15** MI.	2
easy 4 mi.	easy 4 mi.	easy 5 mi.	▶ **21** MI.	3
easy 3 mi.	easy 5 mi.	easy 6 mi.	▶ **22** MI.	4
easy 5 mi.	easy 4 mi.	easy 8 mi.	▶ **28** MI.	5
easy 4 mi.	easy 5 mi.	easy 9 mi.	▶ **37** MI.	6
easy 4 mi.	easy 6 mi.	long 10 mi.	▶ **37** MI.	7
easy 5 mi.	easy 6 mi.	long 10 mi.	▶ **40** MI.	8
easy 6 mi.	easy 5 mi.	long 10 mi.	▶ **40** MI.	9
easy 5 mi.	easy 5 mi.	long 12 mi.	▶ **42** MI.	10

BEGINNER

CONTINUES ↘

Speed, Strength, and Tempo workouts should include a 1.5–3-mile warm-up and cooldown. Weekly total mileage includes a 1.5-mile warm-up and cooldown.

BEGINNER

TABLE 4.1 — HANSONS HALF-MARATHON METHOD: BEGINNER PROGRAM, CONTINUED

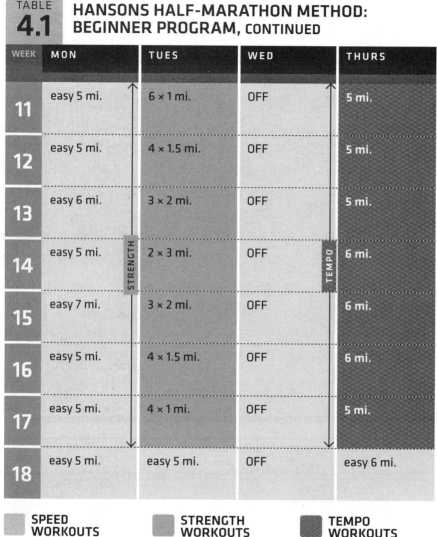

WEEK	MON	TUES	WED	THURS
11	easy 5 mi.	6 × 1 mi.	OFF	5 mi.
12	easy 5 mi.	4 × 1.5 mi.	OFF	5 mi.
13	easy 6 mi.	3 × 2 mi.	OFF	5 mi.
14	easy 5 mi.	2 × 3 mi.	OFF	6 mi.
15	easy 7 mi.	3 × 2 mi.	OFF	6 mi.
16	easy 5 mi.	4 × 1.5 mi.	OFF	6 mi.
17	easy 5 mi.	4 × 1 mi.	OFF	5 mi.
18	easy 5 mi.	easy 5 mi.	OFF	easy 6 mi.

(TUES column: STRENGTH; THURS column: TEMPO)

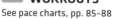

SPEED WORKOUTS
See pace charts, pp. 73–79

STRENGTH WORKOUTS
See pace charts, pp. 85–88

TEMPO WORKOUTS
See pace chart, p. 93

FRI	SAT	SUN	WEEKLY TOTAL	WEEK
easy 6 mi.	easy 5 mi.	long 10 mi.	▸ **44.5** MI.	11
easy 5 mi.	easy 6 mi.	long 12 mi.	▸ **47** MI.	12
easy 6 mi.	easy 5 mi.	long 10 mi.	▸ **45** MI.	13
easy 5 mi.	easy 6 mi.	long 12 mi.	▸ **47** MI.	14
easy 6 mi.	easy 5 mi.	long 10 mi.	▸ **47** MI.	15
easy 5 mi.	easy 6 mi.	long 12 mi.	▸ **48** MI.	16
easy 6 mi.	easy 5 mi.	easy 8 mi.	▸ **40** MI.	17
easy 5 mi.	easy 3 mi.	RACE	▸ **37.1** MI. (INCLUDING RACE)	18

BEGINNER

Speed, Strength, and Tempo workouts should include a 1.5–3-mile warm-up and cooldown. Weekly total mileage includes a 1.5-mile warm-up and cooldown.

The Advanced Program

The Advanced Program is best suited for runners who have completed at least one previous half-marathon. However, if you are a higher-mileage runner and have plenty of experience at shorter distances yet are new to the 13.1-mile distance, you may still be a candidate for the Advanced Program.

It is important to consider your experience. If your past training has involved low weekly mileage plus a high-mileage long run, as suggested by many training programs, you may need to make some adjustments to the Advanced Program; these will be discussed at the end of the chapter. As indicated in the Beginner Program section, some runners who are used to lower mileage may struggle with the Advanced Program due to its aggressive structure and higher volume. That said, a runner who has never completed a half-marathon but is accustomed to 50 or more miles per week will likely thrive using the Advanced Program.

The Advanced Program (Table 4.3) differs from the Beginner Program in several ways, the most obvious being weekly mileage. From the very first week, the Advanced Program doles out more miles, and it continues to follow that trend throughout. While we coach beginners to hit around 45 miles in their peak weeks, advanced half-marathoners are instructed to reach just over 55 miles. It is important to note that the increase in mileage doesn't come from an increase in SOS workouts but instead from ramping up the distance of weekday easy runs. Remember that the easy runs provide a strong stimulus for aerobic development through mitochondrial growth and development, muscle fiber recruitment, and the enhancement of fat use. These benefits are all garnered without the stress that comes along with harder running.

There are also noticeable differences between plans when it comes to the long run. The Advanced Program brings a runner to 14 miles, while the Beginner Program peaks at 12 miles. Too, the structure and buildup are distinct for each of these programs. For instance, a 10-mile run in the Beginner Program is labeled as a long run, but in the Advanced Program it is simply an easy run. Looking at Table 4.2, it is clear that a 10-mile run for a beginner is more significant than for an advanced runner.

TABLE 4.2	COMPARISON OF A BEGINNER AND AN ADVANCED RUNNER FOR A 10-MILE RUN	
SESSION	**RUNNER A: BEGINNER**	**RUNNER B: ADVANCED**
easy pace	9:00/mi.	7:30/mi.
duration for 10-mile run	1:30:00	1:15:00
percentage of weekly mileage	25	18–20

You will also find that SOS workouts begin earlier in the Advanced Program. In the Beginner Program, the runner starts with a base-building period that consists of all easy running; in the Advanced Program, speed workouts begin the first full week, along with the tempo runs. Speed is included early in this program because half-marathon runners are often also training for other races simultaneously. Ideally these races are shorter (such as running a 5K, then a 10K, then your goal half-marathon distance). By doing speed work early, these runners can enter these additional races with a solid fitness level and have a fairly good idea of where they are in their training. When they switch over to the strength segment, they are ready for the race-specific work necessary for their goal half-marathon race.

To get into speed workouts, follow the sequence provided in Chapter 3. Begin with the 12 × 400 workouts, then the 8 × 600s, 6 × 800s, 5 × 1000s,

2-6 min max

TABLE 4.3	HANSONS HALF-MARATHON METHOD: ADVANCED PROGRAM			
WEEK	**MON**	**TUES**	**WED**	**THURS**
1	OFF	OFF	OFF	easy 4 mi.
2	easy 4 mi.	12 × 400	OFF	3 mi.
3	easy 4 mi.	8 × 600	OFF	3 mi.
4	easy 4 mi.	6 × 800	OFF	3 mi.
5	easy 4 mi.	5 × 1K	OFF	4 mi.
6	easy 5 mi.	4 × 1200	OFF	4 mi.
7	easy 5 mi.	3 × 1600	OFF	4 mi.
8	easy 6 mi.	5 × 1K	OFF	5 mi.
9	easy 5 mi.	6 × 800	OFF	5 mi.
10	easy 7 mi.	12 × 400	OFF	5 mi.

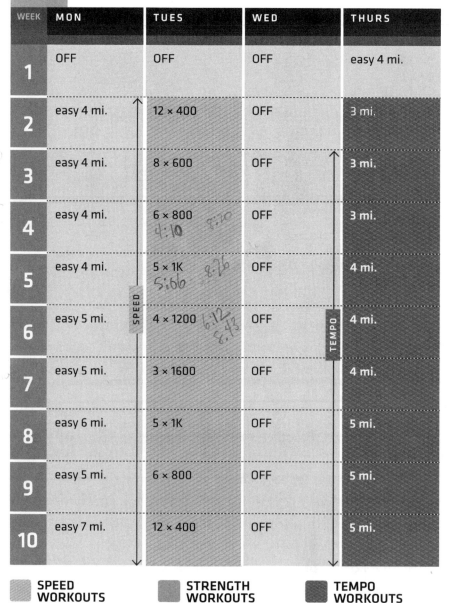

SPEED (vertical label, column TUES)

TEMPO (vertical label, column THURS)

Handwritten annotations: 4:10, 8:20 (week 4); 5:06, 8:26 (week 5); 6:12, 6:43 (week 6)

SPEED WORKOUTS
See pace charts, pp. 73–79

STRENGTH WORKOUTS
See pace charts, pp. 85–88

TEMPO WORKOUTS
See pace chart, p. 93

ADVANCED (vertical tab)

FRI	SAT	SUN	WEEKLY TOTAL	WEEK
easy 3 mi.	easy 4 mi.	easy 6 mi.	▸ **17** MI.	1
easy 4 mi.	easy 4 mi.	easy 6 mi.	▸ **33** MI.	2
easy 5 mi.	easy 5 mi.	easy 7 mi.	▸ **35** MI.	3
easy 4 mi.	easy 6 mi.	easy 8 mi.	▸ **35** MI.	4
easy 5 mi.	easy 6 mi.	easy 10 mi.	▸ **40** MI.	5
easy 6 mi.	easy 6 mi.	long 12 mi.	▸ **43** MI.	6
easy 6 mi.	easy 5 mi.	easy 10 mi.	▸ **41** MI.	7
easy 6 mi.	easy 6 mi.	long 12 mi.	▸ **46** MI.	8
easy 6 mi.	easy 5 mi.	easy 10 mi.	▸ **42** MI.	9
easy 5 mi.	easy 6 mi.	long 12 mi.	▸ **47** MI.	10

ADVANCED

CONTINUES ↘

Speed, Strength, and Tempo workouts should include a 1.5–3-mile warm-up and cooldown. Weekly total mileage includes a 1.5-mile warm-up and cooldown.

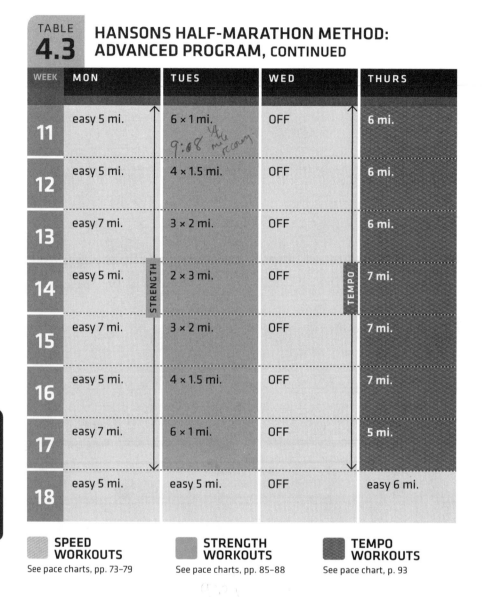

TABLE **4.3**	HANSONS HALF-MARATHON METHOD: ADVANCED PROGRAM, CONTINUED			
WEEK	MON	TUES	WED	THURS
11	easy 5 mi.	6 × 1 mi. *9:08 (handwritten)*	OFF	6 mi.
12	easy 5 mi.	4 × 1.5 mi.	OFF	6 mi.
13	easy 7 mi.	3 × 2 mi.	OFF	6 mi.
14	easy 5 mi.	2 × 3 mi.	OFF	7 mi.
15	easy 7 mi.	3 × 2 mi.	OFF	7 mi.
16	easy 5 mi.	4 × 1.5 mi.	OFF	7 mi.
17	easy 7 mi.	6 × 1 mi.	OFF	5 mi.
18	easy 5 mi.	easy 5 mi.	OFF	easy 6 mi.

SPEED WORKOUTS
See pace charts, pp. 73–79

STRENGTH WORKOUTS
See pace charts, pp. 85–88

TEMPO WORKOUTS
See pace chart, p. 93

FRI	SAT	SUN	WEEKLY TOTAL	WEEK
easy 6 mi.	easy 5 mi.	easy 10 mi.	▶ **46** MI.	11
easy 5 mi.	easy 6 mi.	long 14 mi.	▶ **50** MI.	12
easy 6 mi.	easy 5 mi.	easy 10 mi.	▶ **47** MI.	13
easy 5 mi.	easy 6 mi.	long 14 mi.	▶ **50** MI.	14
easy 6 mi.	easy 5 mi.	easy 10 mi.	▶ **48** MI.	15
easy 5 mi.	easy 6 mi.	long 14 mi.	▶ **51** MI.	16
easy 6 mi.	easy 5 mi.	easy 8 mi.	▶ **45** MI.	17
easy 5 mi.	easy 3 mi.	**RACE**	▶ **37.1** MI. (INCLUDING RACE)	18

ADVANCED

Speed, Strength, and Tempo workouts should include a 1.5–3-mile warm-up and cooldown. Weekly total mileage includes a 1.5-mile warm-up and cooldown.

4 × 1200s, and finally the 3 × 1600 workout. When you get to this point, you have 4 remaining weeks of speed. At that point, work back down the pyramid and do the 4 × 1200s, 5 × 1000s, and 6 × 800s, finishing the last week of the speed segment with the 12 × 400 workout.

In addition to the earlier implementation of speed workouts, the Advanced Program differs slightly in its prescription of tempo workouts. While the Beginner Program jumps from a 3-mile to a 6-mile tempo run, the advanced version goes a mile longer, to 7 miles.

The Just Finish Program

The Just Finish Program was born out of our desire to offer a sound program that would allow even the absolute novice runner a solid program to follow and thus to feel completely confident going into that goal race. This confidence is particularly important if this is your first half-marathon.

Kevin, Keith, and I have worked with a wide variety of runners over the years. One of the biggest and most enthusiastic groups that we coach are charity runners. Their cause is noble, and my work with, for example, the American Cancer Society's Determination team fueled my desire to include this program level in this book. Often, these runners are running not for themselves but for a friend, spouse, or family member. They are doing it for a reason that is bigger than themselves, which earns my respect any day. While this group is the inspiration for the Just Finish Program, the program is also a great option for anyone looking to simply complete the half-marathon distance in a noncompetitive way.

The program operates on a simple premise: The easiest way to increase mileage is to take away the intensity. When you add intensity, you greatly increase the risk of injury. So, the focus of this program is on building a runner's general endurance to a point where the 13.1 miles can be covered safely and with confidence. Put another way, you must build the foundation before starting on the rest of the house. The runner who is using this program needs to completely and soundly build a general endurance foundation before even thinking about walls, a roof, and a sweet infinity pool.

So, when you look at the program, you will see no SOS workouts on Tuesdays and Thursdays. You will see long runs beginning in Week 8; that is one piece of the puzzle that no half-marathon trainee, regardless of experience level, can avoid. The long run is essential to building general endurance especially when the focus is learning to cover ground at a comfortable pace.

Do not overthink this schedule. It is meant to be free-flowing and a learning experience. So, when you follow it, run to some degree by feel. If you feel great one day, go ahead and run a little harder. If you don't feel as good, run slow enough to make sure you can cover the distance. If you went out too fast, slow down, take a walk break—just keep moving! The long runs should be slow and comfortable. Ideally you are building to a point where you can cover the ground without stopping. The true end goal of this program is to provide a building block for something more aggressive or competitive down the line if you so desire, or at least to help you enjoy a positive, fruitful training experience even if this ends up being the only half-marathon you ever do. You should be able to follow this schedule and finish strong at your race. Afterward, we hope you see it as a starting point to a long future of running and competing in races.

TABLE 4.4	HANSONS HALF-MARATHON METHOD: JUST FINISH PROGRAM			
WEEK	**MON**	**TUES**	**WED**	**THURS**
1			OFF	easy 2 mi.
2	OFF	easy 2 mi.	OFF	easy 2 mi.
3	OFF	easy 3 mi.	OFF	easy 3 mi.
4	OFF	easy 3 mi.	OFF	easy 3 mi.
5	OFF	easy 3 mi.	OFF	easy 4 mi.
6	easy 2 mi.	easy 3 mi.	OFF	easy 4 mi.
7	easy 3 mi.	easy 3 mi.	OFF	easy 4 mi.
8	easy 3 mi.	easy 4 mi.	OFF	easy 4 mi.
9	easy 3 mi.	easy 5 mi.	OFF	easy 5 mi.
10	easy 3 mi.	easy 5 mi.	OFF	easy 5 mi.

JUST FINISH

FRI	SAT	SUN	WEEKLY TOTAL	WEEK
OFF	easy 2 mi.	easy 3 mi.	▶ **7** MI.	1
OFF	easy 2 mi.	easy 3 mi.	▶ **9** MI.	2
OFF	easy 3 mi.	easy 4 mi.	▶ **13** MI.	3
easy 2 mi.	easy 3 mi.	easy 5 mi.	▶ **16** MI.	4
easy 2 mi.	easy 3 mi.	easy 6 mi.	▶ **18** MI.	5
easy 2 mi.	easy 3 mi.	easy 6 mi.	▶ **20** MI.	6
easy 3 mi.	easy 3 mi.	easy 7 mi.	▶ **23** MI.	7
easy 3 mi.	easy 3 mi.	long 8 mi.	▶ **25** MI.	8
easy 3 mi.	easy 4 mi.	easy 6 mi.	▶ **26** MI.	9
easy 3 mi.	easy 4 mi.	long 8 mi.	▶ **28** MI.	10

CONTINUES ⬂

JUST FINISH

TABLE 4.4	HANSONS HALF-MARATHON METHOD: JUST FINISH PROGRAM, CONTINUED			
WEEK	MON	TUES	WED	THURS
11	easy 4 mi.	easy 5 mi.	OFF	easy 5 mi.
12	easy 3 mi.	easy 5 mi.	OFF	easy 5 mi.
13	easy 4 mi.	easy 5 mi.	OFF	easy 5 mi.
14	easy 3 mi.	easy 5 mi.	OFF	easy 5 mi.
15	easy 4 mi.	easy 5 mi.	OFF	easy 5 mi.
16	easy 4 mi.	easy 5 mi.	OFF	easy 5 mi.
17	easy 4 mi.	easy 4 mi.	OFF	easy 4 mi.
18	easy 3 mi.	easy 4 mi.	OFF	easy 3 mi.

JUST FINISH

FRI	SAT	SUN	WEEKLY TOTAL	WEEK
easy 4 mi.	easy 4 mi.	easy 6 mi.	**28** MI.	11
easy 4 mi.	easy 5 mi.	long 10 mi.	**32** MI.	12
easy 3 mi.	easy 6 mi.	easy 8 mi.	**31** MI.	13
easy 4 mi.	easy 5 mi.	long 10 mi.	**32** MI.	14
easy 3 mi.	easy 6 mi.	easy 8 mi.	**31** MI.	15
easy 4 mi.	easy 5 mi.	long 10 mi.	**32** MI.	16
easy 3 mi.	easy 3 mi.	easy 6 mi.	**24** MI.	17
easy 3 mi.	easy 3 mi.	**RACE**	**29.1** MI. (INCLUDING RACE)	18

JUST FINISH

Training programs FAQs

In our training clinics, we encounter many of the same questions regarding preparation, year after year. The truth is, we all have similar fears and apprehensions when it comes to taking on a new challenge. As coaches, we have learned through the years how best to answer those questions, sending the runner away feeling more confident about being able to fit in all the training. Whether you choose to subscribe to the Just Finish Program, the Beginner Program, or the Advanced Program, consider the following most frequently asked questions.

WHAT IF I WANT TO SWITCH DAYS AROUND?

We understand that running frequently takes a backseat to work and family responsibilities. While we hope you can bump half-marathon training up the priority list for several months, it's not realistic to expect it to be at the very top. As you may have noticed, SOS workouts are scheduled for Tuesdays, Thursdays, and Sundays. If you are not able to complete a workout on the day it was prescribed, it is okay to switch days around to accommodate your schedule. If you decide to do this, however, make sure that the switch makes sense. For instance, speed workouts are scheduled on Tuesdays. If you know that you are always going to struggle getting those workouts in on Tuesdays because of meetings, kids, or other commitments, change all your speed workouts to Mondays. If you make this change, you should also move back the other workouts, doing your long runs on Saturdays instead of Sundays, and so forth. This keeps the schedule consistent, merely shifting it back, thereby avoiding any alterations in the training itself. The goal is to avoid putting in back-to-back SOS workouts as much as possible because the aim is cumulative fatigue, not reaching the point of no return. If you find yourself in this situation, move your SOS days around to allow for an easy day or a day off in between each.

WHAT IF I WANT TO RUN MORE WEEKLY MILEAGE?

Many runners assume that if they want to increase weekly mileage, tacking miles onto the long run is the obvious choice; however, we caution that tinkering with the long run is the last thing you should do. If you want to add mileage, increase easy days to 10 miles or more or simply run easy on the scheduled off day. For more on this, refer to Chapter 5.

WHAT IF I WANT TO RACE DURING THE TRAINING PROGRAM?

Racing during a half-marathon training program is more feasible than when training for a full marathon. Beginner and new runners are actually encouraged to race at least once, completing a 5K or 10K race to establish a baseline for SOS workouts. For those who already have these baselines but simply love to race, we say go for it. My only caution is to not let other races take away from your training. I have had clients who want to race every week or every other week and who then wonder why their half-marathon was a debacle. The most likely reason is that racing all the time can cause you to miss many of the workouts, which are designed to work in concert and take you to your goal on race day. So racing should be done sparingly enough to satisfy your craving but not take away from the big picture. To alter training for a week: Replace the midweek tempo run with an easy day that was originally prescribed for the weekend. If the race is on Saturday, run easy on Sunday, and then pick up the regular training schedule on Monday. If the race is on Sunday, run easy on Monday. Assess how you feel on Tuesday before picking back up with the schedule. If you feel good enough, do the workout as planned. If not, replace the SOS on Tuesday with a longer easy run, then pick up with the scheduled tempo on Thursday. You may also consider doing your scheduled speed or strength work on Thursday instead of the tempo run (since the race counts as a tempo run), then pick the schedule back up as planned on Friday. You can see how, if you do race too frequently, a whole training cycle can become compromised. For more on this, see Chapter 5.

HOW MUCH SHOULD I WARM UP AND COOL DOWN?

Traditionally we recommend a 1- to 2-mile warm-up and cooldown before and after hard workouts. For most beginners, this takes 15–20 minutes. More advanced runners looking for an easy way to increase weekly mileage may benefit from increasing both the warm-up and the cooldown to 1.5–3 miles.

WHAT IF I WANT TO TAKE A DAY OFF BECAUSE I FEEL TIRED?

If this is the case, you should first determine whether you are injured or simply fatigued. In training, we all experience aches and pains. In fact, many runners just don't feel that great when they're logging high mileage. Feeling somewhat worn-out is a normal and necessary part of the process. If you find you are getting tired, make sure your easy days are truly easy and you aren't cheating your SOS paces down. If you are injured, however, you'll want to consult a coach or physician on what course of action to take.

WHAT IF I DON'T HAVE TIME TO DO THE WHOLE WORKOUT?

This can become an increasing problem as the tempo runs get longer and the strength workouts begin because, at this point, training requires more of your time. If there just aren't enough hours in the day, do what you can. Remember, something is always better than nothing. If the schedule shows a 10-mile tempo run but you have time for only 6 miles, then do 6 miles. You'll certainly garner greater benefits from doing a 6-mile tempo run than from doing nothing at all.

WHAT IF I WANT TO SWITCH MY WORKOUT DAYS AROUND?

The most frequent requests I get are to move the tempo workout to Friday or the speed/strength workout to Monday, or the off day to some other day. It's perfectly fine to make these changes. The training plans schedule the day off on Wednesdays because Wednesday was traditionally clinic day during our fall marathon program. These clinics were held in the evenings, which meant most people had to choose between either doing a run or attending the clinic. To sidestep this conflict, Wednesday became the programs' day off from running. If this does not work for you, however, feel free to move workout days around. The only rule is to have at least one rest or easy day between SOS days. A common switch is doing the tempo run on Friday to have another day of recovery between that and the speed/strength workout on Tuesday. That's a simple switch because it only requires that you reverse the Thursday and Friday runs, without adjusting anything else.

5

Program modifications

WHEN I WROTE MY first book, *Hansons Marathon Method*, I wasn't married, had no kids, and had all the time in the world to focus on writing. Now, a couple years later, I juggle coaching, running, writing, and quality time with my wife and young daughter. It's downright chaotic at times. I'm no different than most of you, so I certainly realize how hard it can be to make time to train along with all that we have going on in our lives. A great support system helps. And a good program, and coach for that matter, should be reasonably flexible, recognizing that life happens while we train and that sometimes runs need to be moved around or adjusted. A good program will allow for such adjustments with minimal overall "damage" to the person's training. Let's discuss some of the common issues that come up and how you can work around these to make the Hansons Half-Marathon Method work for you.

Increasing weekly mileage

Our programs fit a wide range of time goals and abilities; however, we still receive some requests for information on how to add to the weekly volume. As we have discussed, the faster a runner wants to complete the half-marathon, the more training he or she will have to put in (to a point). That added training generally comes in the form of an increase in weekly mileage. If you are a first-time half-marathoner following the Just Finish Program, you are probably better off sticking with the recommended mileage for your first 13.1-mile training journey. If, on the other hand, you have never raced the half distance but have some experience with shorter race distances, the Beginner Program probably has the right mileage for you. It will give you that all-important increase in weekly mileage without throwing too much at you at once. Even if you have been successful in shorter races, running high mileage is an entirely different beast. So if you haven't run high weekly volume, give the Beginner Program a shot for your first half-marathon and then slowly add mileage or move up to the Advanced Program for your second attempt at the distance, depending on how your body responds.

If you are experienced in the half-marathon distance and are following the Advanced Program, adding mileage becomes a bit more complicated. While the intuitive choice may be to add to the long run, we first suggest running on your rest days to add mileage. If you are looking to ramp up your weekly mileage, we recommend adding an easy 4–8 miles on Wednesday, your rest day, and voilà! You instantly see roughly a 10 percent increase in mileage. For many runners, an easy running day, rather than a rest day, placed between the two SOS days may actually better stimulate recovery and uphold the routine.

Another approach for adding mileage is through the modification of easy days in the Advanced Program, most of which have runs of 4–6 miles. It is reasonable for an experienced half-marathoner to increase those runs to 6–8 miles. By adding 2 miles to each easy run during the week, you bank an additional 8 miles per week, topping you out in the 60 miles per week range. We have successfully used this approach with a number of competitive men and women who run in the low 1:30s and sub-1:30-hour range.

A final method for adding mileage to the Advanced Program is to increase the distance of the long run. We don't recommend throwing in an 18- or 20-mile long run just for the sake of doing it, however. With the half-marathon distance, the rules remain in line with our overall philosophy, which means keeping your long run at 25–30 percent of weekly mileage and less than 3 hours. Your longest long run is already longer than the race distance, so being able to cover the ground on race day should not be a concern. However, our programs offer plenty of room between where the long runs sit and where they could max out if you have already increased your weekly mileage by using the other ideas just discussed.

For the ambitious few who have slowly increased their mileage and are looking to safely hit that 70–80 miles per week range, we again suggest adding miles to easy days, making those runs at least 10 miles each. If you run all 7 days per week, with 4 easy days, that will total 40 miles per week, or 40–50 percent of your goal. In this scenario, strength workouts total 11 miles, and we usually recommend adding a 3-mile warm-up and cooldown before and after to log a few extra miles. Including the warm-up and cooldown, tempo runs will peak at around 13 total miles, and we suggest increasing the Saturday run to 6–10 miles. Then, when you add in an 18- to 20-mile long run, you've got about 95–100 miles on your legs for the week. However, unless you are looking at running a half-marathon in the sub-1:15 range, these changes are probably not realistic.

Runners will also often ask us about running twice a day. As with the long run, our recommendation depends on the person. For most people, it's hard enough to find time to run once a day, let alone twice.

If you are looking to add up to 10 miles per week, then it's usually easier to just add Wednesday as an easy run. Then you are left with only a few miles to account for, and it's simpler to just add a mile to a run a couple of times during the week. For those running 70–80 miles per week, an 8- to 10-mile run will take anywhere from an hour to 80 minutes (e.g., 10 miles @ 8:00/mile). For people who are running that sort of mileage and looking to finish in 1:05–1:20 in the half-marathon, a 10-mile run is not a major run. Even in this scenario, a second run may still not make a lot of sense. In this case, easy runs of 8–10 miles added to the SOS will already put you well into the 70–80 miles per week range. After a person is running more than 10 miles a day, however, two runs per day should be considered. At that point you are talking about 14–15 miles, or more, per day. It may not seem like much, compared with 10 miles of single runs, but at this level, those 4–5 extra miles put in during a second run can elicit real physiological adaptations.

In Appendix A, we discuss the plan followed by the elite athletes in the Hansons-Brooks Distance Project. Here you can garner some ideas on how higher weekly volume can be broken up. To reach the coveted 100-mile mark, you can either increase your easy runs from 10 miles to 12 miles, which will give you an extra 6 miles per week, or you can add a second 4-mile run a couple of days a week. All this mileage is added without messing with the volume or intensity of the core SOS workouts, demonstrating what huge gains added easy mileage can spur on its own.

Adjusting for races

One of the most common reasons runners require a change in their training program is to accommodate races. While we generally suggest including other races sparingly leading up to a half-marathon, in certain situations such competitions are advantageous. In particular, we have discussed the benefits of beginners racing a 5K or 10K to help establish a baseline for their half-marathon-specific training. For this race to be useful, you must schedule it strategically. For a number of reasons, the first and best opportunity is at the end of Week 7 in any of the programs. The first 4 weeks are spent increasing base mileage to prepare you to handle harder-intensity running; this is followed by the speed segment of training, along with increasing mileage. Because it takes about 3 weeks to adjust to new training stressors, it makes sense to schedule a race at that 7-week point. With the Just Finish Program, a race gives you an opportunity to see where your fitness is at and decide if you want to establish a time goal.

As far as race planning around your half-marathon, I would suggest a 5K during the speed cycle and a 10K during the strength cycle. That way, you are (1) building your race distance throughout the training cycle and (2) racing a distance that won't take away from your other training. A 5K during the earlier training weeks would be about what your Thursday tempo run distance would be. During the later stage of the training block, a 10K would be around the tempo distance. So, you get to race and not lose out on an SOS day.

The training grid (Table 5.1) demonstrates more specifically how you might shift around your workouts to best accommodate a race. You'll notice that during the week, Thursday's tempo run is replaced by Saturday's easy run, while the Friday run remains the same. Saturday is then race day, which replaces the tempo run. This is a strategic replacement because both a race and a tempo run stimulate the anaerobic threshold. Hence, the Sunday run is replaced by another easy run that is longer in duration. Beyond that week, the schedule picks up again right where it left off.

This example and the previous discussion in Chapter 4 demonstrate why it is important not to race too often, regardless of whether you're

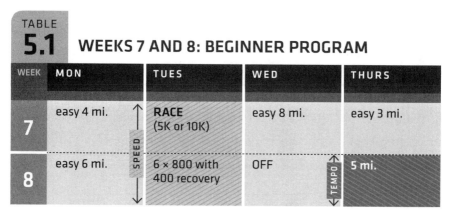

TABLE 5.1	WEEKS 7 AND 8: BEGINNER PROGRAM			
WEEK	MON	TUES	WED	THURS
7	easy 4 mi.	RACE (5K or 10K)	easy 8 mi.	easy 3 mi.
8	easy 6 mi.	6 × 800 with 400 recovery	OFF	5 mi.

Example of placing a race within a training week during the speed section of the Beginner Program.

using the Just Finish, Beginner, or Advanced Program. Races cause big adjustments in the tempo runs, long runs, and sometimes both. While the impact is not as strong early in the training, it becomes a larger issue the closer you get to your half-marathon. Each runner has to weigh his or her own pros and cons of racing sparingly or often. If you are not overly concerned with your finish time in the half-marathon, then the number of times you race beforehand matters less. On the other hand, if the half is your ultimate goal and you are chasing a time, then you want to choose races sparingly, paying close attention to their timing in your training program.

Adjusting for conflicts

Prior to any structured training, many runners are fairly haphazard in their approach to running, putting in varying amounts of volume and intensity depending on mood, weather, and the like. While any exercise is obviously good for your body, training requires more focus and strategy. Herein lies one of the greatest challenges in following a structured training program: scheduling conflicts. For instance, your child's T-ball

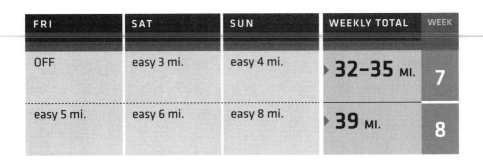

FRI	SAT	SUN	WEEKLY TOTAL	WEEK
OFF	easy 3 mi.	easy 4 mi.	▸ **32–35** MI.	7
easy 5 mi.	easy 6 mi.	easy 8 mi.	▸ **39** MI.	8

games are on Thursdays, the same day you are supposed to do your tempo workouts. Or maybe you have to work every Sunday, which is also the scheduled long run day. As coaches, we find ourselves reassuring runners about these issues every marathon cycle. By giving you three simple guidelines for working around life's obligations, we offer you the tools to tend to your responsibilities without letting your running get off track.

GUIDELINE 1: MAINTAIN REGULARITY IN TRAINING

If you decide to switch your workouts around, stay as consistent as possible. For instance, if you trade Thursday's workout for Friday's one week, try to do the same every week moving forward. The key is to avoid constantly swapping different days every week. If you move your strength workout to Friday one week, but then do another strength workout the following Tuesday, you've done two strength workouts within a 5-day period. This not only upsets the training balance but also can lead to injury and overtraining. If you know something is going to regularly conflict on a certain day of the week, make sure the changes are uniform across weeks and months. If you work all day Sunday, switch your long runs to Saturdays throughout the entire training cycle. Routine is the key here. The more you can maintain it, the better.

GUIDELINE 2: ENSURE REST DAYS AND EASY DAYS REMAIN IN PLACE

Put simply, you should always take either an easy day or a rest day between SOS workouts. If you miss your speed workout on Tuesday and complete it on Wednesday instead and then go right into your tempo run on Thursday, you're asking for an injury. In this situation, the best bet is to move the tempo run to Friday, leaving an easy run on Saturday and a long run on Sunday. This shows that you can adjust for certain obligations and disruptions without upsetting the entire balance of training.

GUIDELINE 3: SOMETHING IS ALWAYS BETTER THAN NOTHING

Consider the previous example in which an SOS workout was missed on Tuesday. What's a runner to do if there is no other possible day to reschedule the workout later in the week? One option is to just move on. That's right, cut your losses and move on to the next SOS workout. In some circumstances, there may be no way around this scenario. If you don't have time to get in the full workout, however, the other option is to consider sneaking in a quick run, or abbreviating the workout, getting in what you can. Even a 25-minute run is better than forgoing a workout altogether.

Adjusting for illness or injury

Illness and injury are certainly the most frustrating reasons you may need to adjust your training around. Over the weeks to months you spend preparing for the 13.1-mile distance, you are likely, at the very least, to catch a bug. The chance of injury, on the other hand, is largely avoided through smart training, but it is not entirely eliminated. Even when you're doing everything right, you can trip on a curb and take a spill or roll an ankle on uneven terrain. Here is how to navigate these potential running layoffs, depending on the number of days missed and when these days are missed.

1 TO 2 DAYS MISSED

Maybe you tweaked your knee or were sick in bed for a couple of days. If you come out unscathed after a day or two, training can resume normally without scaling back mileage or intensity. You just lose a couple of days of running—no harm done. For example, if you took a wrong step at the end of your long run on Sunday, causing you to miss training on Monday and Tuesday, simply jump back in on Wednesday. If you are feeling 100 percent, complete Tuesday's SOS workout on Wednesday and move the Thursday tempo to Friday. This allows you to still fit in all of the week's SOS workouts, but it also adheres to the rule of scheduling an easy or rest day between hard runs. However, if you aren't able to reschedule your SOS days to fit within those parameters, then just forge ahead with your tempo run on Thursday and let go of the missed SOS workout. While a number of missed workouts can spell doom for your marathon goals, a single lost workout will never be your demise.

3 TO 6 DAYS MISSED

Physiological regression will be minimal, even if no running at all takes place within this time frame. Usually, a person who misses this many days has something more than a 24-hour flu or a simple ache or pain. With that said, if you are feeling healthy enough to get in a couple of short, easy jogs while you recuperate, by all means do so. If instead you're truly laid up, rest assured that the consequences of a few days off won't deter your end goal. After 3–4 days of missed training, come back slowly by running easy for 2–3 days, then pick the schedule back up and follow it as usual. If you have missed 5–6 days, run easy for 3–4 days and then revert to the previous week's training regimen. After that week, jump ahead and catch back up with the training program. For instance, if you miss Week 3, run easy through Week 4 and then return to Week 3's workouts during the 5th week. After that, jump to Week 6 and follow the training as it was originally prescribed.

7 TO 10 DAYS MISSED

At this point the body starts to lose some of those hard-earned physiological gains you have made. You've probably heard the saying "You lose it twice as fast as you gain it." It always seems that it takes a lot more time and effort to gain fitness than it does to lose it. Taking a week and a half off from running definitely necessitates serious schedule modification; however, that modification depends on the point in the plan at which the missed block occurs. If it occurs before the strength portion of the training program, then the runner won't have to make any major adjustments to race goals. If the setback happens after the strength workouts begin, the runner will probably need to adjust race goals because there may not be enough time to get in all the normal training. Keep in mind that if you can still manage to run some short, easy runs during this period and have the go-ahead from your doctor, the time it takes to return to normal training will be significantly less. If running isn't possible, commit to crosstraining to prevent a drop-off in fitness. The hope is that fitness will remain high enough to allow an easier and faster transition back to healthy running. Always remember in these situations to consult a physician who is familiar with runners before diagnosing yourself and prescribing your own treatment. In either case, you don't need to abandon your plans to run the half-marathon, but adjustments are necessary.

Upon your return to running, you should run easy for the same number of days that you missed. If you lost a week, then run easy for a week. After that, go back to the last training week that you were able to complete and repeat it, then run the week that was originally missed, and from there pick the schedule back up. So, with a week missed, it takes 3 weeks to get back on track. If you are able to run easy during your time off, subtract a week from that time frame. This advice applies throughout the training program, but once strength workouts have begun, you may do the math and realize, "Wow! I don't have enough time." Unfortunately, this happens. While many people can rebound quickly enough to run the race, their goal time will be compromised. Once you get into that final 4–6 weeks of training, the pros and cons of racing should be weighed. If you are really looking to run that goal time and you miss 10 days of running with 5 weeks to go, you could choose to look at other race options. If you are comfortable with potentially missing the mark, then go for it.

MORE THAN 10 DAYS MISSED

Unfortunately, if you are forced to miss this much time, you are faced with a serious decision. After 2 weeks of lost training, the decreases in physiological gains are quite significant—as much as 3–5 percent. While this might not seem like much, consider this: For a runner attempting a 2:00-hour half-marathon, a 4 percent loss means an increase of nearly 5 minutes for the overall finishing time. The slower the race goal time, the more time gained. Even worse, after 21 days away from running, 10 percent or more of fitness is forfeited. This means that VO_2max and blood volume can decrease by up to 10 percent, anaerobic threshold decreases significantly, and muscle glycogen decreases by as much as 30 percent. These are all important to endurance performance, and if you miss 2 weeks of running, it may take more than 2 weeks to even get back to your previous level, setting you far off course. In particular, if this happens during the strength portion of the program, there simply may not be enough time to regain your fitness levels and get ready for the goal race. If you are following the Just Finish Program, you don't have a designated strength portion, but you will still be in the hardest part of your training at this time, so the guidelines here are still applicable.

Although you won't run your best, advanced runners in this situation may be able to sneak in shorter training segments and still complete the race, albeit likely falling short of the original time goals. However, beginners and first-time half-marathon runners should be cautious when it comes to losing substantial amounts of training time and forging ahead to the goal race. For runners in this situation, consider choosing a new race or at least revising time goals. In all our years of coaching, we've seen too many people rush back from illness or injury to make a race deadline, often forgoing proper recovery and in the end having a poor race experience.

If you are set on running the originally scheduled race, be sure to step back and understand what the time off from running means for you physiologically. If you've taken 2 weeks off, adjust your race goal by 3–5 percent. If you've missed closer to 3 weeks, adjust your expected performance by 7–10 percent. For example, if Runner A missed 2 weeks of training and was shooting for a 2:00 half-marathon, she should adjust her goal by 3.6 minutes (120 × 0.03) to 6 minutes (120 × 0.05). The new time goal would then be 2:03–2:06. Any more than 4 weeks off, and we suggest choosing a new race altogether.

DOWNTIME DISCRETION

Although we have just presented a number of ways to modify your training schedule, we contend that it is best to avoid taking unscheduled days away from training if at all possible. This applies even when your legs are tired and sore, since soreness and injury are not inextricably linked. There will be times during training when your legs are achy, fatigued, and nonspecifically sore; it just comes with the territory. Many of the adaptations that happen during training occur as a result of running on the days you just don't feel like running.

If you have an injury, however, your response should be different. For less severe injuries, make sure that you are not only taking time off but also using that time to identify the root cause of the problem. Otherwise you may continue to run into the same issue upon returning to training. For instance, if you are experiencing shin splints, figure out what you need to do to reduce the pain, like getting new shoes or implementing a strength routine. If your body will allow it, reduce the volume and intensity, but continue running short and easy through the healing process. While training may need to be reduced, it doesn't necessarily have to stop completely to allow for recovery, that is, if the cause of the injury is identified and treated. When you can maintain some fitness, downtime is significantly minimized, and regular training can be resumed much sooner.

PART III
the
strategy

6

Selecting
race goals

BY THIS POINT IN the book, you have learned about the different training programs and chosen the one that best suits your experience and objectives. Congratulations! That is half the battle! However, once you've decided which training program you are going to follow, it's time to identify your race goals. Goals vary among runners, but it's important to set a goal that is in line with what half-marathon training demands. Some runners simply hope to finish the race, some want to cross it off their "bucket list," and some are looking to run as a means of raising money for charity. On the other end of the spectrum are runners hoping to maximize what they can get out of their body, run as fast as possible, or earn a place on the podium. The beauty of this sport is that all these athletes begin on the same starting line—from those who promised themselves to lose a little weight all the way to someone chasing down a world record. The common factor is that they all have a goal for that race, and it affects how they train.

Borrowing from the business world, we suggest setting SMART goals: goals that are specific, measurable, attainable, realistic, and timely. A specific goal is one that is defined and clear-cut, so rather than stating that you hope to finish a half-marathon, you identify an actual time goal. (If you follow the Just Finish Program, a precise time goal isn't necessary, but if you can get an idea of the time you would be happy running, it gives your runs more purpose.) By setting a measurable goal, such as 1:45, you give yourself a definite objective. You also want to be sure that your goal is attainable. While a 1:45 half-marathon may be within reach for someone who previously ran a 2:00, it may not be for someone who holds a 2:45 personal record (PR). Similarly, a realistic goal is one that considers your physical abilities and scheduling constraints. If you are only going to have time to train 4 days a week, it is unlikely you'll be able to achieve a 1:40 half-marathon. Finally, a timely goal is one that is contained within a specific time frame. This one is easy because you automatically have the period between the start of the training plan and the moment the gun fires at your chosen race. By following the SMART criteria, you are more likely to achieve your predetermined objectives going into a race.

In a perfect world, we would encourage runners new to the 13.1-mile distance to set smaller goals before considering a half-marathon. When runners slowly move up the race ladder from a 5K, to a 10K, to a half-marathon, they build their aerobic capacity and tolerance to increased training volumes. What's more, the shorter races provide a solid baseline for half-marathon training, giving feedback for what a reasonable race goal might be.

If you are looking to simply cross the finish line by any means necessary, then the Hansons Just Finish Program is probably the best fit for you. This program is far more loosely structured than the other plans, but that doesn't mean you will be taking it easy. You will be running solid weekly mileage and building your general endurance. A great goal for those following this program is not only to get across that finish line but to do so feeling as strong as possible. A time goal isn't mandatory, but I encourage developing a loose time goal as the program progresses. Having some sort of time goal will help you gauge if you are running too fast or too slow during your daily runs, in comparison with what you would like to attempt on race day.

On the other hand, the Beginner Program and the Advanced Program are more focused and structured. By nailing down a specific time goal within one of these programs, you are able to identify precisely how you should train in order to achieve that mark. More than training you to just make it across the finish line, we give you the tools to execute the half-marathon distance successfully, while also leaving your love for running and hunger for competition intact. The goals you set will give you a starting point for training by guiding your workouts and providing a tangible target to shoot for throughout your half-marathon preparation.

Time goals can be determined in various ways. Sometimes, runners seek a qualifying time for a certain race, such as a time that will gain them access to a desirable start line corral at a major half-marathon. This is the easiest type of goal to pinpoint because the standard is already set. For runners who have previously completed the half-marathon distance, a new PR is another popular time goal. We also frequently hear from many runners who want to break the big barriers, such as the 3:00-hour, 2:00-hour, and 1:30-hour marks. While we encourage you to set the bar high, make sure your goal is manageable and keeps you engaged in your training. There are several guidelines to consider as you zero in on a SMART half-marathon goal.

Goal-setting guidance

CURRENT TRAINING AND PAST TRAINING

Your goals should be contingent on your current foundation of training. For instance, someone who has been injured for the past 6 months will set different goals than someone who has been consistently running 50 miles per week during that same period. In the same way, the goals of a beginner will vary dramatically from those of a seasoned half-marathon racer.

CURRENT PERSONAL BEST

If you have previously run a half-marathon on relatively low training mileage, even a slight uptick in miles will probably lead to great jumps in your personal best. However, if you are a 1:30 half-marathoner who has been running 50–60 miles per week, improvements will be less substantial. Consider these numbers: A 5 percent improvement for a 2:00 half-marathoner is about 6 minutes, which would get that runner under the 1:55 mark. The same percentage of improvement for a 1:10 half-marathoner is about 3:30 minutes, which would bring that person from being competitive on a regional level to being a borderline national-class runner. Obviously, that 5 percent improvement means different things, depending on one's pace.

TRAINING AND AVAILABILITY

The time you devote to training has a significant effect on the quality and volume of the training and, thus, the final result. When choosing a goal, look realistically at how much time you'll have available to train. Time determines not only how hard and long you can train on a day-to-day basis but also how consistent you can be over a long period. For example, a runner can perform quite adequately in local 5Ks or 10Ks by logging 25–30 miles per week, perhaps running 3 days with a long run of 1 hour. While this works for shorter distances, this person would likely struggle to get in adequate training for a half-marathon on that same timetable. With the half-marathon distance, the recommended mileage is 30 miles per week for a less seasoned, slower runner and 40–50 miles per week for faster runners.

TRAINING WINDOW

The length of time until your goal race will offer some guidance in goal setting. If you are a newer runner or new to the half-marathon distance, plan for a longer buildup period before you attempt 13.1 miles. Having a base of miles is important in helping you start your training strong. The Beginner Program and the Just Finish Program do have a few weeks built into the front end that allow you to build a small base. For veterans who train consistently, however, the half-marathon-specific training can be shorter because you have an established mileage base. This assumed base is why in our Advanced Program, SOS days begin right away in the training plan. Some runners prefer a slower buildup; others choose a short, intense training segment.

EXTERNAL FACTORS

When setting your half-marathon goal, keep in mind that outside factors such as terrain, temperature, and race size all have the potential to affect your performance on race day. If you are accustomed to training in cool, dry conditions, but your chosen goal race is likely to be hot and humid, adjust your final time goal. Also check the course profile; you might want to predict a slightly faster time on a flat course and a somewhat slower time on a course with an abundance of hills. Finally, if you are running a large half-marathon and find yourself stuck behind a large crowd in one of the last corrals, you may want to tack on a few extra minutes. Even though your chip won't begin timing until you cross the start line, your time may be affected by a slower mass of runners in front of you.

How to use a race equivalency chart

A race equivalency chart (Table 6.1) is a particularly handy tool for a runner looking to pinpoint a realistic time goal based on current ability. This chart allows you to take a recent race time and see what an equal performance would be for an alternate distance. Instead of simply multiplying your pace at a shorter distance by 13.1, you can use this chart to obtain an "equal performance" prediction. As an example, according to the chart, if you ran a 23:00-minute 5K, you should be able to run a 1:46:19 half-marathon. Because pace naturally slows with distance, the chart suggests what you'd probably be capable of in an equal performance at a longer distance. If you have run only marathons to date, use your marathon time and backtrack to see what your half-marathon time would potentially be. Be sure not to confuse this with a pace chart, which shows you what a certain pace will equal for a given distance, such as the 5K, 10K, half-marathon, and marathon.

If you don't have a race time logged, another option is to complete a field test by doing a time trial on a track. To do this, complete a short warm-up as you would before any SOS workout. Then run 1 mile as fast as you can at a steady, hard pace. Following your cooldown, find your time on the race equivalency chart and check what might be a reasonable time goal for the half-marathon. The longer the race or time trial, the more accurate the half-marathon prediction is going to be. Unsurprisingly, a 10K will be a better determinant than a 1-mile time trial. The best way to figure out an appropriate goal is to plug in several times from varying distances and find the range that they put you in.

I have known a few runners who couldn't use shorter race distances as predictors because they could hold very close to their best 5K pace all the way up to the half-marathon distance. Every runner is different, so if you have several times available from different distances, you will be able to more accurately predict a finishing time in the half-marathon.

Regardless of the goal time, be sure to select it before you begin the strength segment of the training program, which is when most of the half-marathon-specific training is completed. That time goal provides a tangible number on which to base those SOS workouts.

Adjusting goals

Although race equivalency charts are helpful, some runners find they need to adjust their goal time once they get into training. If you over-estimated what you'd be capable of on race day, you'll know for certain once you get into longer tempo runs and strength runs. When you're struggling to run a 6-mile tempo run at goal pace, it is safe to assume that the pace will be too tough to hold for another 7 miles on race day. In this case, it is best to adjust your goal time to a slightly slower finish to ensure that you have confidence going into the race.

At the other end of the spectrum, some runners will want to set the bar higher once they begin their SOS workouts. Perhaps you originally thought a 2:00 half-marathon was reasonable, but workouts are going well, and you now think 1:45 would be a more appropriate goal. This situation is tricky. While we like to encourage runners to pursue their greatest potential, we also don't want to set them up for failure. If you become overzealous in your training, you risk overtraining and injury, which means you might not even get to the starting line, much less the finish. If you initially would have been satisfied with your original time goal at the outset of training, why jeopardize training by entering into

TABLE 6.1 RACE EQUIVALENCY CHART			
MILE	**2-MILE**	**5K**	**10K**
12:59	27:43	45:00	1:33:29
12:16	26:10	42:30	1:28:17
11:32	24:38	40:00	1:23:06
11:24	24:19	39:30	1:22:03
11:15	24:01	39:00	1:21:01
11:06	23:42	38:30	1:19:59
10:58	23:24	38:00	1:18:56
10:49	23:06	37:30	1:17:54
10:40	22:47	37:00	1:16:52
10:32	22:29	36:30	1:15:49
10:23	22:10	36:00	1:14:47
10:14	21:52	35:30	1:13:45
10:06	21:33	35:00	1:12:42
9:57	21:15	34:30	1:11:40
9:48	20:56	34:00	1:10:38
9:40	20:38	33:30	1:09:35
9:31	20:19	33:00	1:08:33
9:22	20:01	32:30	1:07:31
9:14	19:42	32:00	1:06:28
9:05	19:24	31:30	1:05:26
8:56	19:05	31:00	1:04:24
8:48	18:47	30:30	1:03:21
8:39	18:28	30:00	1:02:19
8:30	18:10	29:30	1:01:17
8:22	17:51	29:00	1:00:15
8:13	17:33	28:30	59:12
8:04	17:14	28:00	58:10
7:56	16:56	27:30	57:08
7:47	16:37	27:00	56:05
7:39	16:19	26:30	55:03
7:30	16:00	26:00	54:01
7:21	15:42	25:30	52:58

15K	10-MILE	HALF-MARATHON
2:24:51	2:36:38	3:28:01
2:16:49	2:27:56	3:16:27
2:08:46	2:19:14	3:04:54
2:07:09	2:17:29	3:02:35
2:05:33	2:15:45	3:00:16
2:03:56	2:14:00	2:57:58
2:02:19	2:12:16	2:55:39
2:00:43	2:10:32	2:53:20
1:59:06	2:08:47	2:51:02
1:57:30	2:07:03	2:48:43
1:55:53	2:05:18	2:46:24
1:54:17	2:03:34	2:44:06
1:52:40	2:01:49	2:41:47
1:51:03	2:00:05	2:39:28
1:49:27	1:58:21	2:37:10
1:47:50	1:56:36	2:34:51
1:46:14	1:54:52	2:32:32
1:44:37	1:53:07	2:30:14
1:43:01	1:51:23	2:27:55
1:41:24	1:49:38	2:25:36
1:39:47	1:47:54	2:23:18
1:38:11	1:46:10	2:20:59
1:36:34	1:44:25	2:18:40
1:34:58	1:42:41	2:16:22
1:33:21	1:40:56	2:14:03
1:31:45	1:39:12	2:11:44
1:30:08	1:37:28	2:09:26
1:28:31	1:35:43	2:07:07
1:26:55	1:33:59	2:04:48
1:25:18	1:32:14	2:02:30
1:23:42	1:30:30	2:00:11
1:22:05	1:28:45	1:57:52

CONTINUES ⌐

TABLE
6.1 RACE EQUIVALENCY CHART, CONTINUED

MILE	2-MILE	5K	10K
7:13	15:24	25:00	51:56
7:04	15:05	24:30	50:54
6:55	14:47	24:00	49:51
6:47	14:28	23:30	48:49
6:38	14:10	23:00	47:47
6:29	13:51	22:30	46:44
6:21	13:33	22:00	45:42
6:12	13:14	21:30	44:40
6:03	12:56	21:00	43:37
5:55	12:37	20:30	42:35
5:46	12:19	20:00	41:33
5:37	12:00	19:30	40:30
5:29	11:42	19:00	39:28
5:20	11:23	18:30	38:26
5:11	11:05	18:00	37:24
5:03	10:46	17:30	36:21
4:58	10:37	17:15	35:50
4:54	10:28	17:00	35:19
4:50	10:19	16:45	34:48
4:45	10:09	16:30	34:17
4:41	10:00	16:15	33:45
4:37	9:51	16:00	33:14
4:32	9:42	15:45	32:43
4:28	9:32	15:30	32:12
4:24	9:23	15:15	31:41
4:19	9:14	15:00	31:10
4:15	9:05	14:45	30:38
4:11	8:55	14:30	30:07
4:06	8:46	14:15	29:36
4:02	8:37	14:00	29:05
3:58	8:28	13:45	28:34
3:53	8:18	13:30	28:03

15K	10-MILE	HALF-MARATHON
1:20:29	1:27:01	1:55:34
1:18:52	1:25:17	1:53:15
1:17:15	1:23:32	1:50:56
1:15:39	1:21:48	1:48:38
1:14:02	1:20:03	1:46:19
1:12:26	1:18:19	1:44:00
1:10:49	1:16:34	1:41:42
1:09:13	1:14:50	1:39:23
1:07:36	1:13:06	1:37:04
1:05:59	1:11:21	1:34:46
1:04:23	1:09:37	1:32:27
1:02:46	1:07:52	1:30:08
1:01:10	1:06:08	1:27:50
59:33	1:04:24	1:25:31
57:57	1:02:39	1:23:12
56:20	1:00:55	1:20:54
55:32	1:00:02	1:19:44
54:43	59:10	1:18:35
53:55	58:18	1:17:26
53:07	57:26	1:16:16
52:19	56:34	1:15:07
51:30	55:41	1:13:58
50:42	54:49	1:12:48
49:54	53:57	1:11:39
49:05	53:05	1:10:30
48:17	52:13	1:09:20
47:29	51:20	1:08:11
46:41	50:28	1:07:02
45:52	49:36	1:05:52
45:04	48:44	1:04:43
44:16	47:52	1:03:33
43:27	46:59	1:02:24

uncharted territory? Especially with race day nearing, ramping up training can spell disaster for a runner. Always remember: You'll run a better
race slightly undertrained than you will overtrained. In fact, many times
the greatest battle is just getting to the start line feeling healthy and fresh.

Other types of goals

In addition to your overall time goal, you may have other small goals
you want to reach along the way. For instance, many of the runners who
attempt one of our half-marathon programs have never run 30, 40, or 50
miles per week; if this applies to you, your first incremental goals might
be simply to hit those marks. Reaching a weekly mileage goal can be
a huge motivator, especially when you are fatigued and questioning
why you're doing this in the first place. You can also set goals related
to supplemental training (discussed in detail in the following chapter).
Many runners find motivation in setting targets for their crosstraining, stretching, and resistance training routines. These goals may be as
general as "I'm not going to skip any days of running in the training
program" or "I'm going to stretch after every workout." The higher your
ultimate time goal, the more important these variables become.

In the same way you should use the SMART goals strategy for your
race day goal, it can also be utilized to set your smaller goals along
the way. Be sure these goals are specific, measurable, attainable, realistic, and timely. Goals of any sort narrow your focus and give meaning
to your training. Without them, runners are left to their own devices,
which can send training into a haphazard spiral. Give your goals some
serious consideration and begin by setting the small goals that will
help you achieve that ultimate time goal.

7

Supplemental training

BY NOW, YOU'VE PROBABLY realized that we like mileage and we like running most days of the week. To run your best half-marathon, you need to run. It is that simple. This philosophy is hard on those runners who like to spend as much time doing other activities as they do running. We get that. But remember, this plan is a commitment you make for 18 weeks. When a goal is important, you make the time to do it right. All that said, as mentioned earlier, there is a time and rationale for including other activities in your race training. There are other pursuits, such as crosstraining, flexibility, and strength training, that you can do in smaller quantities to boost performance and prevent injury. The main idea here is that this additional training should be supplemental to and not a replacement for the running. You want to focus on activities that support your training rather than hinder it; therefore, you have to be careful about what supplemental work you include. Implementing an appropriate amount of crosstraining, along with a bit of flexibility and strength work, however, can better your running performance, by allowing you to work on certain weaknesses that may be limiting your running potential, and also add variety to your training.

Crosstraining

While crosstraining attracts a lot of attention in sports media, the Hansons Method limits its inclusion. The reasoning is simple: The most direct path to becoming a better runner is through running. This notion follows a basic principle of physiology known as the rule of specificity. The idea is that your body adapts specifically to the stress it is placed under. A 30-minute swim is great for general fitness, but it doesn't translate directly into good running performance.

So while crosstraining isn't a major component in our programs, it can play a small but significant role in race preparation. The most obvious reason to include alternate exercises is for rehabilitation after injury. If you find yourself injured, supplemental exercises can get you back on your feet faster by providing a reduced-weight-bearing activity, thereby allowing for increased blood flow to the injured area to promote tissue repair. Additionally, they help maintain cardiovascular fitness, which assists in your return to running. Indeed, sitting on the couch waiting for something to heal isn't the answer.

The key to crosstraining during injury is to find an activity that mimics running as closely as possible, such as using an elliptical or a stationary bike. While options like the rowing machine may provide a great cardiovascular workout, the emphasis is placed on the upper body and won't help the running muscles. It should be noted that the protocol can vary based on the specific injury. If you have a broken foot, for instance, biking will only aggravate the ailment further. Be cognizant of whether the activity affects the injured area and steer clear of anything that causes pain. That said, an antigravity treadmill can allow people with stress fractures to run, and do so safely. These can often be found at local sports clinics; if there is one in your area, I'd suggest checking it out.

Another instance in which we might recommend crosstraining is during periods of planned downtime away from running. For the half-marathon, it's likely you won't need two full weeks off following your race, which is what we normally prescribe for after a full marathon. However, the appropriate recovery time is highly individual. A person leaping out of his or her comfort zone to make it through a half may require a solid 10 days off, while a veteran runner may be able to get away with 5 days. The Hansons-Brooks team athletes take some sort of planned break after all of our training segments. Planned recovery works wonders for the body! A hiatus can give runners time to restore damaged muscles, rejuvenate the spirit, and plan the next move. Crosstraining offers the opportunity to enhance that recovery by providing a way to continue burning calories and maintain some of the fitness gained during half-marathon training.

We are often asked about how many half-marathons a person can or should run in a year. Again, the answer tends to be highly individual. For instance, those who were brand new to running at the beginning of half-marathon training may not want to do a second one for a very long time. They may prefer to return to shorter races and build their overall fitness before making the decision to move up to the half again. Veteran runners with more miles on their legs than their cars may decide to make three or four quality attempts at a half-marathon in a year. The beauty of the half distance is that you can race it and still run pretty well at 5Ks and 10Ks during your training.

The final reason we might prescribe crosstraining is to provide a beginner runner a means through which to ease into the sport. For a person who has never run or isn't already active, there is a limit to how many days he or she can safely run, at least at the onset of training. Initially, this may be only 15 minutes at a time, 2 or 3 days a week. In this situation, it is important to fill the other days with workouts on an elliptical or a bike, or even a walk. As general fitness improves, these crosstraining days can gradually be replaced with running. For most true beginners, it can take several months to transition into running 5–6 days per week.

We always tell runners in our training programs to consider their previous experience with a crosstraining activity and to stay away from new exercises until after the goal race. While you may be feeling fitter than ever during training, be sure to temper that zeal for exercise. You are already under enough physical stress leading up to your half-marathon; adding a new activity to the mix just increases risk of injury and threatens to derail your focus. Runners most commonly want to add in crosstraining on Wednesdays, their day off from running. While cycling or Pilates is great for your health in almost every other circumstance, these activities, being less productive and potentially harmful, may only hinder recovery from running. If you always ride your bike to work and have been doing so for years, by all means continue your routine, within reason. In this case, your body has already adapted to that exercise. If it is a long ride, however, consider taking the bus on SOS workout days. If you were a Pilates enthusiast before beginning hard training, you should cut down your practice but not necessarily eliminate it. Just remember: Don't start anything new until after the goal race.

The other guide to deciding whether or not to cross-train is your body itself. If you are having trouble recovering from running workouts, you definitely shouldn't be piling on supplemental training. In addition, if you think you may be overtraining, replacing running with a crosstraining activity isn't the answer either. If that is the case, you would benefit more from a day off so you can return to running feeling fresh the following day. We occasionally encounter runners who claim that they simply can't handle higher mileage and therefore need to cross-train. Before automatically sending them to the elliptical to replace running mileage, I take a hard look at the paces they are running, the shoes they are wearing, the races they are doing, and anything else that could potentially be sabotaging their running. More often than not, it is a training issue. It has been our experience that if the training schedule is controlled for how fast you are running, as the Hansons plans are, then the mileage will take care of itself. Put another way, many people mistakenly hammer their mileage in programs with shorter overall volume, which then limits their ability to adapt to higher mileage. Once in a while, a person just can't seem to adapt to running mileage no matter what he or she does. If you find yourself in this boat, step back and weigh the pros and cons of your half-marathon goal. With that said, over the years we have encountered far more runners who struggle to remain healthy on programs that recommend low mileage and lengthy long runs than on the moderate weekly mileage and moderate long run volumes offered by the Hansons Method.

Flexibility

Although stretching has been linked to the sport of running since the jogging craze of the 1970s, the topic is more complex than most people realize. By itself, flexibility refers to the maximal static (not moving) range of motion for a particular joint. The more flexible a person is throughout his or her joint range of motion, the easier it is to stretch the corresponding muscle. This makes for a more elastic muscle that is less prone to injury, but it also means the muscle can't create as much power as a less elastic muscle. Imagine a Stretch Armstrong doll; the more you pull his arm, the wimpier-looking he gets. In the same way, the farther you stretch a muscle, the less elastic power it will have to fire. This is where active range of motion becomes important. This type of flexibility is conducted through a set of active movements that target the running joints and muscles. To properly implement a flexibility routine, you must understand the difference between these two types of stretching and when to utilize them. While there has been conflicting research over the years, the latest and most convincing evidence suggests that there is a time and a place for both active (dynamic) and static stretching. For both performance and injury prevention, it is important to do the right type of stretching at the right time.

DYNAMIC STRETCHING

This form of flexibility training involves rhythmic movement throughout a person's full range of motion. These motions are deliberate and controlled. One type of active stretching, often referred to as ballistic stretching, is fast-paced and bouncy, taking the joint beyond the natural range of motion. This can be fairly dangerous and put you at risk for injury, so we generally suggest avoiding ballistic movements. Dynamic stretching, in contrast, focuses on proper form and motions that help to actively increase range of motion within reasonable parameters. When performed after a warm-up and prior to a speed, strength, or tempo run, dynamic stretching benefits a runner in a number of ways. First and foremost, the dynamic movements reduce muscle stiffness, which decreases the risk of muscular injury. They also help prepare the body to run faster by loosening you up without stretching your muscles to the point of reducing their power. In fact, dynamic stretching can actually stimulate fast-twitch and intermediate fibers that often get neglected during traditional run training. The other advantage of this type of stretching is its influence on training the brain and the muscles to work in concert by engaging the muscle fibers and the nervous system simultaneously.

To best put dynamic stretching into practice, warm up for 1–3 miles before a high-intensity workout and then perform several of the following exercises. They should take no more than 10–20 minutes and are an easy way to improve your entire workout. Pick and choose the exercises you like best and perform them in any order you prefer.

1 arm swings

Standing tall with feet shoulder-width apart, swing your arms in a circular, clockwise motion, mimicking propeller blades on each side of your body. Avoid crossing your arms over your chest. Keep your back straight and knees slightly bent. After 6–10 repetitions, swing the arms from the sides across your chest in a back-and-forth motion for another 6–10 repetitions. These exercises help relax the major upper-body muscles, making your upper body more efficient during running. This is particularly advantageous because runners tend to carry tension in their arms and shoulders, which affects the rest of the stride.

2 side bends

Standing tall with feet shoulder-width apart and hands on the hips, lean smoothly from left to right, being careful not to lean backward or forward. As you lean, raise the hand from the opposite side above your head. Repeat 16–20 times. These bends will assist in keeping the spine mobile.

3 hip circles

Standing tall with feet shoulder-width apart and hands on the hips, begin by making circles with your hips, leaning as far forward and backward as comfortably possible. Perform 10–12 rotations in a counterclockwise motion and then reverse direction for another 10–12 rotations. By opening up the hips, this exercise allows for a better range of motion in your stride.

4 half-squat

Standing tall with feet shoulder-width apart and hands on the hips or straight in front of you, bend at the knees as shown, then slowly straighten your legs to return to the starting position. Perform 10–12 times. The half-squat can help develop a higher leg lift, which improves your natural stride and helps you avoid shuffling and other inefficiencies.

5 leg kicks

Stand with your left side next to a wall, placing your weight on your right leg (outside leg) and your left hand on the wall. Swing your left leg forward and backward in a pendulum motion for a total of 10–12 repetitions. Reverse position and do the same with your right leg.

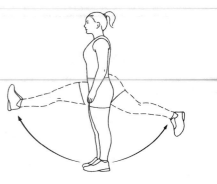

6 leg swings

Stand facing a wall with both hands on the wall. Swing your right leg across the front of your body. Swing it as far to the left as you can move comfortably and then back to the right as far as you can move comfortably. Do 10–12 times and then switch legs.

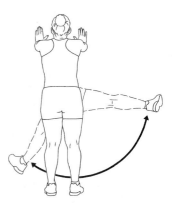

7 slow skipping

Skip slowly for 30–50 meters, or 10–15 seconds. Turn around and skip back to your starting position.

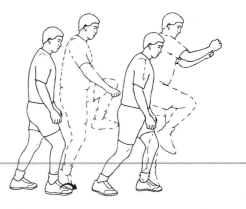

8 high knees

Following a straight line, jog slowly and focus on lifting your knees toward your chest in a marching fashion. Pay attention to driving the knee toward the chest and also consider proper arm carriage and pumping rhythmically with the opposite knee. Proper arm carriage has arms bent at 90 degrees and moving back and forth as if on a pendulum at the shoulder. The up-and-down actions should be quick, but your movement forward should be steady and controlled. Travel down and back, 30–50 meters in each direction.

---

9 butt kicks

In this reverse motion of high knees, pull your heels back rapidly toward your buttocks. Again, the motions should be quick, but your linear movement steady. Travel 30–50 meters, turn, and continue back to your starting position.

🔟 cariocas

Also known as the "grapevine," this is the tricki-
est of the exercises in terms of coordination. You
can stand with your arms perpendicular to your
torso or, if more comfortable, with arms bent at
your side. Stand with feet shoulder-width apart.
Moving to the left, pull your right foot behind the
left. Step the left out to the side. Then cross the
right leg in front of the left and again step the
left to the side. Basically, the legs twist around
each other while the torso remains still on the
twisting pelvis. Travel 30–50 meters, turn, and
continue with these steps as you travel back to
your starting position.

⓫ bounders

These are a similar motion to the high knees, except instead of driving the
knees high into the chest, the focus shifts to pushing off with the trailing leg
and driving forward. It is a cross between a skip and high knees. Travel
30–50 meters, turn, and continue these steps back to your starting position.

⑫ sprints

At the end of your exercise routine, do 4–6 repetitions of a 75- to 100-meter sprint at near-maximal effort. Always do your fast running with the wind, so jog back against the wind to start a new sprint. The sprints shouldn't be more than 15 seconds, so slower runners should begin with 75-meter sprints.

The name of the game for exercises 5–12 is muscle engagement. By actively engaging the muscles and getting the neuromuscular connections firing, you are (1) preparing your body to run fast, (2) working on specific running motions that will aid in proper form development, and (3) developing a neuromuscular connection to fast and intermediate muscle fibers that will serve as a major advantage late in the half-marathon when your slow-twitch fibers are fried.

STATIC STRETCHING

When most people talk about stretching, they are referring to static flexibility. Unlike dynamic stretching, static stretching is done standing or sitting still, rather than using an active motion. For years, runners have performed static stretching routines before workouts and races. Ironically, this is probably the worst time for this activity, since it reduces muscle force production by stretching the muscles out too much. The muscles lose their elasticity as they are stretched, making them less powerful and also putting you at risk for a muscle tear. Even so, there is a place for static stretching in your training toolbox; you just have to know when and how to use it.

There has been much research to support the use of static stretching after workouts as a means of injury prevention. For instance, calf tightness has been shown to be associated with pronation of the rear foot, which causes the tibia and fibula (lower leg bones) to internally rotate, resulting in a pain that is commonly referred to as shin splints. More specifically, this kind of inflexibility can lead to tendinitis, stress fractures, Achilles tendon injuries, and knee issues. Poor flexibility also tends to cause the front of the pelvis to tilt forward, creating excessive curvature in the lower back. The result is a tightening of the lower back muscles, which predisposes the runner to back injuries.

While crosstraining and dynamic stretching can be utilized periodically, static stretching should be done on a regular basis to avoid these issues. Keep in mind that the research shows it takes a minimum of 3 weeks of "regular" stretching before improvements are seen, which often means doing such exercises every day, sometimes twice a day.

Over time, a static stretching routine will help you gain and maintain better all-around flexibility, promote injury recovery, and improve running form, as well as relaxing the muscles and promoting maximal range of motion.

The following stretches should be performed post-run, holding them for 20 seconds and doing 1–3 repetitions each. Never stretch to the point of pain or until the muscle shakes; keep each movement slow and controlled. These stretches should be incorporated into your daily routine, taking about 10–15 minutes after your run. If you are in a post-run rush, the stretches can be done later in the day or evening, just not prior to a run.

① low back

Lie flat on your back. Draw both legs toward the chest. For a stretch, place hands behind knees and pull knees close to the chest. This stretch will isolate the long back muscles that run from the pelvis to the shoulder blades.

② shoulder

Stand upright with feet shoulder-width apart. Pull the right arm across the front of the body so that the arm is perpendicular to the torso. With the left hand on the elbow (or slightly above—toward the shoulder), gently pull the right arm toward the left side. Repeat with the left arm. Much of the tension we carry ends up in the shoulders. Because many runners begin pulling their shoulders up when they get tired, poor form can result. If you have a tight shoulder carriage to begin with, it can affect the way your arms swing, which will affect your running efficiency.

❸ chest

Standing upright facing an open doorway, place feet shoulder-width apart. One foot should be slightly in front of the other for balance. With your arms straight out from the body (you should look like a T), place your arms against the wall on either side of the doorway, palms touching the wall. Lean forward until you feel a gentle stretch in the pectoral muscles and biceps. Many runners tend to have very tight chest muscles that cause them to roll their upper back (like a hunchback). This stretch helps prevent poor posture and form that can lead to inefficient running.

❹ calves

Begin by standing a foot or two away from a wall and lean forward so your hands are bracing you against the wall. With the left foot stationary and bent, slide the right foot back another 12 inches. The right heel should be kept on the ground. As your chest gets closer to the wall, slightly bend the right leg to stretch the other calf muscle. Repeat for the left leg. Added flexibility in the calf muscles helps you to avoid potential pronation and tendon problems.

5 gluteal

Lie on your back on a soft, flat surface. Bend the left leg so that the knee is pointing upward but the foot is still flat on the floor. Next, fold the right leg and rest the ankle of that leg on the left knee. The right leg should be perpendicular to the left leg. With your hands interlocked at the back of your left thigh, pull the left knee toward the chest as far as you comfortably can. Repeat on the opposite side.

6 groin

Start by standing upright with your feet more than shoulder-width apart. Lower the right hip in a squatting fashion, bending the right leg and keeping the left leg straight. For balance, place hands on the right knee, if you wish. You should feel the stretch along the inside of the left leg. Switch sides and repeat.

7 hamstrings

Sit on a soft, flat surface with legs extended in front of you. Bend the left knee so that the bottom of the left foot rests along the inside of the right thigh. The right leg should be straight out from the body with a very slight bend at the knee. Slowly bend forward from the waist so that the stretch is truly focused on the hamstring muscle group and not the upper back. Repeat with the right leg.

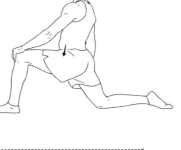

8 hip flexors/quads

Start by standing upright with your feet more than shoulder-width apart. Lower the right hip in a squatting fashion, bending the right leg and keeping the left leg straight. For balance, place hands on the right knee, if you wish. You should feel the stretch along the inside of the left leg. Switch sides and repeat.

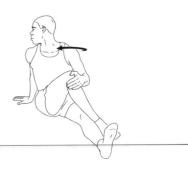

9 hips

Sit on the floor with the left leg extended to the front. Cross the right leg over the left leg. The right foot will be on the outside of the left leg. Next, place the left arm so that the hand is on the outside (right side) of the right knee. The right arm should be a brace, positioned on the floor near the hip. Finally, twist to the right by using the left arm as a lever against the right leg. Repeat on the opposite side.

The purpose behind stretches 5–9 is identical. The muscles in the pelvis are used for stability, but they can also limit range of motion. If these muscles are tight, the natural stride length is diminished, leading to a decrease in running economy. By keeping these muscles flexible and allowing for free range of motion, you maximize your natural stride length.

Strength training

Strength (resistance) training is a form of supplemental work that some runners choose to utilize. Increased strength contributes to better running in a number of ways. First and foremost, it helps to improve form, especially in the upper body. It also can assist in preventing injuries through the protective effects of stronger muscles. Additionally, strength training helps to fight fatigue by training the body to be able to draw from fast-twitch fibers late in an endurance event.

A number of exercises belong under the strength training umbrella, including the drills described in the previous section, core muscle training, and free weights. I often hear that runners avoid strength training because they are worried about putting on "bulk" and gaining weight. In reality, it is fairly difficult to add any significant muscle mass onto your body weight. If the right exercises are done in the correct volumes, the average runner won't have to worry about putting on extra pounds.

Although there are many options for adding strength training to a running program, our basic philosophy involves three main ideas: (1) It complements the running regimen; lifting or other strength work should never replace running. (2) It helps correct weaknesses, muscle imbalances, and poor running form; in essence, strength training should help to improve running performance. (3) It is short and simple; not only does redundancy occur when you commit yourself to a long, complicated strength routine, but you also take away valuable time from the real goal, which is running. We understand that many people following this training plan work full-time and have many other responsibilities. As a result, the exercises provided here are easy to do on your own without a gym membership or fancy equipment. Simply choose two or three of these exercises to do after easy running days.

❶ crunch

Begin by lying on your back with your knees bent so that your feet are flat on the floor. Contract your abdominal muscles to pull your trunk up. Many people use momentum to carry themselves up or use their legs to push off and roll upward, but this does not provide the desired strength work. Instead, focus on small movements from abdominal contractions. The total movement during the crunch may only be a few inches. Start off with 3 sets of 10, progressing to 3 sets of 25 over the course of several weeks. At that point, increase either the number of sets or the number of repetitions per set. The goal is to strengthen the abdominals, which are essential in maintaining running form and posture. Having strong abdominals makes it easier to tuck the pelvis underneath your body, improving stride through better body positioning.

2 back extension

Lie facedown on the floor, with the majority of your weight on your stomach. Extend both legs about shoulder-width apart, and extend your arms straight in front of you. You want to maintain a nearly straight line from your fingers to your toes. Finally, contract the lower back muscles and square off your shoulders so that your entire back is straightened. Hold for 2–3 seconds and release. Repeat 12–15 times. During running, the back absorbs a lot of force upon each foot strike; the stronger the back is, the better it will handle it.

3 superman

The Superman is similar to the back extension, but instead of simply contracting the back muscles in a stationary position, you lift one arm and the opposite leg. Lying facedown on top of an exercise ball, lift your left arm and right leg at the same time (you can't lift both sides without rolling off the ball). This strengthens the arms, glutes, and back in one shot. Hold each contraction for 1 or 2 seconds before releasing. Repeat 12–15 times on each side. Having a strong upper back means less shoulder slouching, promoting proper posture and upper-body running motion.

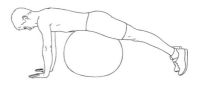

4 bridge

Lie on the floor with both legs bent so that your heels are touching the floor. Rise up by contracting the glutes, back, and hamstring muscles. When this is done properly, you will be able to draw a straight line from the tops of your bent knees to your head. Hold each contraction for 1–3 seconds and perform 12–15 repetitions. As this becomes easier, you can try a one-legged version, with one leg bent and the other leg straight and raised off the floor (as the bent leg is contracted). This is intended to strengthen the glutes and hamstrings, which are often weaker than the quads due to running. It also stretches the notoriously tight hip flexors.

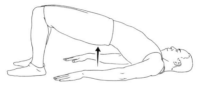

5 side plank

Lie on your right side. Then bend your right arm so that the humerus bone, or the bone between the shoulder and elbow, is the "post" and your forearm is perpendicular to the rest of the body. Your right foot should rest on the floor with your left foot on top of it. Raise your body off the floor. Don't sag in the midsection or bend at the waist. Again, straight lines should be seen in all planes. Hold the position for 10–20 seconds and increase the time as you get stronger. This exercise helps to balance strength between the front and side abdominal muscles.

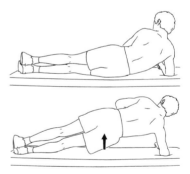

Together, these strength exercises offer an all-encompassing intro-duction to resistance training. Consider adding some to your running regimen, and you'll surely notice a difference in a matter of weeks. While running can take up much of your time, strength training is a quick and easy way to potentially boost performance and ward off injuries.

Final thoughts on stretching and flexibility

Consistency is the key to success with stretching and strength train-ing. If you do the exercises described here only once every few weeks, there's no benefit to be gained. In fact, it just makes you more fatigued with no return on investment. So, if you chose to follow a strength and flexibility program, be consistent. Start with 1–2 days per week for sev-eral days. Start with 1–2 sets of these exercises. After several weeks, assess where you are and add a day or add a set if that feels appropri-ate. Slowly adjust the workload to the point where you simply want to maintain and not advance. Finally, start early in your training block or before it rather than throwing either of these into the middle of a training block.

8

Nutrition and hydration

WHEN I WAS 25, like many other twentysomething men and women, I paid little heed to proper hydration and nutrition. I ate and drank what I wanted or whatever was available, assuming that if I just trained hard, my races would be fine. Sometimes they were but sometimes they weren't, and I know now that if I had considered details like nutrition, I could have counted on more consistent and probably better results. Now, older and just slightly wiser, I have learned firsthand how intricately related all of these elements are. Training, performance, diet, and hydration are closely intertwined. If you are off on one, the others will suffer; what's worse, your true potential will remain an unknown.

Fueling for the half distance differs from fueling for the marathon because the degree to which it affects your race depends more on your pace. In a shorter, faster run, there is less risk of physically running out of fuel unless you have started with a low tank to begin with. However, runners trying to crack a 3-hour barrier have to consider their fueling a lot like a marathon runner would because they are in it for the long haul and face the serious risk of "bonking," or running out of stored carbohydrate, before they reach the finish line.

Speed aside, diet matters. Whether you are a performance-based athlete or are out there for fun and health, diet trends will certainly affect you, for better or worse. So, no matter what your situation is, having a baseline of nutritional education is a very useful weapon in your arsenal. While general recommendations are provided here, it is important to seek out advice from a physician or sports nutritionist for individualized guidance if you have a specific concern.

Nutrition: Fueling to go the distance

Hard training requires consideration of three important aspects of nutrition: consuming enough calories, consuming the right calories, and consuming calories at the right times. Once you have these three things figured out, you'll be well on your way to building an optimal base of fuel for training and racing.

CONSUMING ENOUGH CALORIES

Training for a half-marathon is a major undertaking, and your caloric needs will be different than during periods of inactivity or casual exercise. By taking in the appropriate amount of calories, you'll maintain a healthy weight and support your training. Large calorie deficits can sabotage your training and performance, leading to issues such as overtraining, illness, and injury. More important, overall health can be jeopardized. The athletes who are afraid of eating too much tend to also be the ones who end up feeling burned-out or injured, often as early as 6 weeks into hard training. This is not a coincidence, of course, so ensure you are monitoring your calories and taking in a sufficient number for your level of training.

Even if you are looking to lose a bit of weight during endurance training, now is not the time to start a calorie-cutting diet. Generally speaking, hard training alone tends to lend itself to slight weight losses over the long term, without introducing any major dietary shifts. Remember that in order to do that training in the first place, your body requires the proper fuel to stay up and running. Consequently, skipped meals and severe calorie restrictions (reductions of 1,000 calories or more) will greatly impede your training and should be avoided. Such unhealthy diets will keep you from running your best on a daily basis, diminishing your race performance.

Those who are running more for fitness than for a top race time can consider coupling exercise with slight dietary restrictions. Remember, however, that caloric deficits should be slight and weight loss will be slow. These adjustments can be safely made while completing half-marathon training, although I strongly recommend seeking out professional advice to help you perform well, stay healthy, and lose weight all at the same time.

Calculating caloric needs

Here are two quick formulas that give you an idea of how many calories (technically kilocalories, but we will use calories here) you need on a daily basis. They are simple to use and accurate enough to give you a general range indicating what is appropriate for you based on body weight and level of exercise.

1. Light to moderately active (45–60 minutes of moderate activity, most days of the week)

body weight × 16–20 cal./lb. = daily calories

TABLE 8.1	SERVING RECOMMENDATIONS BY VARIOUS CALORIE LEVELS		
	1,800 CAL.	**2,000 CAL.**	**2,200 CAL.**
grains	11 oz.	12 oz.	13 oz.
fruits	2 cups	3 cups	3 cups
vegetables	2 cups	2 cups	2 cups
milk/yogurt	2 cups	2 cups	2 cups
protein	6 oz.	6 oz.	8 oz.
fats	4 tsp.	4 tsp.	5 tsp.

It's important to consider not only how many total calories to consume but also how to divvy up those calories.

2. Very active (60–120 minutes of moderate exercise, most days of the week)

body weight × 21–25 cal./lb. = daily calories

For example, here is a caloric range for a 150-pound runner who engages in 60 minutes of easy running per day:

150 lb. × 16 cal./lb. = 2,400 cal.
150 lb. × 20 cal./lb. = 3,000 cal.

This runner should consume between 2,400 and 3,000 calories per day. We provide these two formulas with the expectation that you will use both of them over the course of training because you will need to consume more calories on your long run day than you will on a short,

2,400 CAL.	2,600 CAL.	2,800 CAL.	3,000 CAL.
14.5 oz.	15.5 oz.	16 oz.	17 oz.
3 cups	3 cups	3 cups	4 cups
3 cups	3 cups	3 cups	3 cups
2 cups	2 cups	2 cups (milk) 1 cup (yogurt)	2 cups (milk) 1 cup (yogurt)
8 oz.	9 oz.	10 oz.	10 oz.
5 tsp.	6 tsp.	7 tsp.	7 tsp.

easy day. Let the length of your run be your guide in choosing the equation that will yield the number of calories you should consume on that particular day. Don't obsess over these numbers; they are meant to give you a general idea of the number of calories you should be consuming. Over time, you'll internalize approximately how many calories you should take in and won't need to continue referring to the equations. If you weigh yourself regularly and at a similar time each day, you will see trends in your weight over time. Use those trends as your guide to caloric consumption.

Having worked with runners of various ages and levels of experience, we find that most people tend to overestimate how many calories they need. Generally speaking, males should use the middle to higher end of the ranges, while women should refer to the middle to lower end. We often get the question from aging runners, "Since I'm older, should I be consuming fewer calories?" Again, generally speaking, men will typically need to cut their caloric consumption by 10 calories for every year of age past 20, and women should do so by 7 calories per year. These recommendations are based on what happens physiologically in the context of a population that tends to become increasingly sedentary with age. If activity levels remain high throughout life, caloric modification can be minor.

Of course, it is not just about hitting a calorie number. Table 8.1 gives you a general idea of how your caloric intake should be broken down into a healthy, runner-friendly diet, indicating how much you should be eating from the major food groups on a daily basis. As you get into training, extra calories will come from sports drinks, bars, or gels that you are consuming before, during, and after major workouts. While easy running days don't require such nutritionals, longer SOS workouts (more than 8 miles) are the perfect staging ground to experiment with your race day fueling plan. During these more race-specific workouts, you'll have the chance to determine which gels, chews, beans, or drinks work best to keep your body running.

CONSUMING THE RIGHT CALORIES

Knowing how much to eat is only part of the picture. As you may have guessed, not all calories are created equal. The numbers may be the same, but the residual effects from eating 700 calories at a fast-food joint will vary considerably from consuming 700 calories of home-cooked food sourced from a local farmer's market. Later in the chapter, we will discuss more specifically what foods to eat and how best to time consumption, but first let's take a general look at the three sources from which our bodies draw for energy: carbohydrates, fats, and protein. All are important for different reasons and, in the right amounts, will keep you properly fueled for everyday excellence.

Carbohydrates

When it comes to endurance nutrition, carbohydrates dominate the discussion, as they should your diet, accounting for 60–70 percent of it, to be exact. Over the last few years, however, they have received a bad rap, as more than a few folks have tried to cash in on our country's obsession with dieting, specifically the promotion of low-carbohydrate regimens. It turns out, however, that the conversation is somewhat misguided. To be sure, there is no denying that we are in the midst of an obesity epidemic, placing a major burden on people's health as well as our nation's economy. It is also true that simple carbohydrates have largely contributed to this problem. But here's the caveat: There are two different types of carbohydrates, simple and complex, and only one of them is detrimental to a person's health when consumed in excess. Simple carbohydrates come from refined grains, soda, candy, and other processed foods, while complex carbohydrates are contained in vegetables and whole grains such as oatmeal and brown rice. Both types of carbohydrates should play a role in the diet of an endurance athlete and will directly impact performance, but your main focus should be on fruits, vegetables, and whole grains.

QUICK-GRAB CARBS
ripe banana
whole-grain spaghetti
apple
cereal
skim milk
berries (strawberries, blueberries, raspberries, etc.)

By emphasizing complex carbohydrates, you will get the energy you need, as well as a number of important vitamins and minerals.

Carbohydrates are a necessary part of an endurance athlete's diet for a number of reasons. From the perspective of performance, carbohydrates are utilized much faster than fat and protein. That is why at increased exercise intensities, carbohydrates become the sole fuel source by allowing the body to continue producing energy through anaerobic means once we have reached our VO_2max. Meanwhile, fat is used only at lower intensities because it can't keep up with high-energy demands, and protein is relied upon when carbohydrate stores are exhausted. Carbohydrates also aid in water absorption, so when you're taking in fluids during a long run, the carbohydrates will actually help the stomach empty faster, allowing the body to more efficiently utilize water. This means that fluids and carbohydrates reach their final destinations more quickly, and the faster they get there, the less likely you are to run out of energy and hit the wall.

Importance of carbohydrates for exercise:

- // provide energy, especially at higher intensities
- // aid in water absorption
- // serve as primary fuel source for your brain and nervous system

Carbohydrates are also the primary fuel source for your brain and central nervous system. That foggy feeling or inability to focus late in a race generally stems from rapidly depleting glycogen (carbohydrate) stores. What's more, carbohydrates play a role in metabolism. Maybe you've heard the saying "Fat burns in the flame of carbohydrates." Basically, by limiting your intake of carbohydrates, you may also limit your ability to burn fat. While not proven, the theory holds that the processes, or pathways, that carbohydrates and fats go through to provide energy result in certain by-products that are necessary for fat to be metabolized. From what I have seen, the major processes will still occur, but about 20 percent of the process ends up unaccounted for. Or, we can state that energy metabolism of fat relies on carbohydrates to be present in order to work at a high rate of efficiency. The point to take away here is that one thing can't replace another, and because carbohydrates are the limited source, they become the most likely to break down the cycle. Finally, the storage of carbohydrates is very limited, making them especially important to replenish on a daily basis. They account for a large portion of your recommended dietary intake because, without carbohydrates, you wouldn't be able to train consistently, much less run a good race.

Besides all these important functions, carbohydrate stores play a tangible role in your running performance. Consider the fact that between the liver, muscles, and bloodstream, your body can store only around 2,000 calories' worth of carbohydrates. Your body utilizes those carbohydrate stores when exercising at even moderate intensities, but it begins to burn through them more rapidly as intensity increases. Refer back to Figure 2.2, and you'll see that at 60 percent intensity, the average person is burning about 50/50 between fat and carbohydrates. Because we have extremely limited carbohydrate stores, and half-marathon pace is somewhere between 60 and 85 percent of maximal capabilities, you can see that if we are burning 100 calories per mile, then at least 50 calories per mile are coming from carbohydrates. With faster runners (with finishing times of 90 minutes or faster), glycogen depletion is less of a worry, but they still burn it quickly because of their high intensity level. For 2- to 3-hour half-marathoners, glycogen depletion can be a risk because they are running a long way and at a pretty high intensity. To make matters more complicated, the body first burns through the carbohydrate (glycogen) stores in the muscles. Altogether, the muscles store about 1,500 calories, but only the muscles that are being used will actually burn that glycogen; unfortunately, our body doesn't allow one muscle to borrow glycogen from another muscle. For instance, the quadriceps won't be able to access glycogen from the trapezius muscles. So, even though running requires the quads to work harder, thus depleting the associated glycogen stores, they can't simply borrow unused glycogen from the less hardworking traps. You may have 1,500 calories' worth of glycogen stored in your muscles, but you won't be able to access all of it, decreasing the amount of usable glycogen even further.

On top of all of this, the glycogen stored in the liver is reserved for your brain and central nervous system. The amount in the blood is even lower than what the liver has to offer, so don't count on that source taking you very far. The phrase "hitting the wall" refers to the point where you've become reliant on your blood sugar to assist the running muscles, meaning you're running on an empty tank. Plainly put, proper carbohydrate consumption provides the foundation of your nutritional training plan. Many half-marathon runners won't be in serious jeopardy of completely running out of carbohydrate stores during their race; hitting the wall, or bonking, occurs much more commonly in the marathon distance. However, those runners who are covering the 13.1 miles in 2, 3, or more hours may face running out of fuel at some point. Regardless of training level, without those building blocks, your body will not tolerate any significant volume of mileage or level of intensity.

Fats

Fats are a necessary part of a balanced diet, especially when you consider the large quantity of fat that our body stores. If you strictly limit your fat intake, either you're not eating enough in general or you're forced

QUICK-GRAB "GOOD" FATS
walnuts, pecans, almonds
nut butter
canned white tuna
avocado

to eat other nutrients all day long in order to feel satiated. Because fat has about twice as many calories per gram as carbohydrates, a little bit of fat will go a long way toward keeping you feeling full. Fat is also involved with the structure of cell membranes and spinal cord tissue, which can have a direct effect on physical performance. Finally, fat is essential because it helps the body absorb vitamins A, D, E, and K, all of which are necessary for optimal health.

In addition to contributing to overall wellness, fats lend a hand in supporting your endurance training and running performance. As your endurance increases, the mitochondria within the muscles grow and become denser, which consequently gives you the opportunity to produce a greater amount of aerobic energy. This is the point at which both fats and carbohydrates can be utilized. Once the exercise intensity reaches 85 percent or higher, however, there isn't enough oxygen available to allow fat to be burned, so carbohydrates become the primary source. The good

Importance of fats for exercise:

// abundant source of energy that spares carbs

// an increasingly better fuel source as your fitness improves

// location of crucial vitamin absorption

// involved in cell structure

news is that, while the average person switches to burning carbohydrates at around 60 percent of maximal intensity, endurance training can bring that percentage up a few extra points.

This means that your body will be able to burn fat at a higher intensity before carbohydrates take over. In practical terms, you'll be capable of running a little bit faster for a little bit longer. Despite this, we still don't need to eat large amounts of fat. For the best results, your diet should include about 20 percent fats, coming from sources such as nuts, fish, seeds, and avocados and limiting fatty meats and other sources of saturated fat.

Protein

Protein should make up the smallest amount of your diet, about 10–15 percent. It plays a major role in repairing damaged muscles after running and also serves as an energy source. When you get to the point of drawing from those protein stores, however, it's a last-ditch effort to stay up and running. Additionally, protein assists in the manufacture of enzymes, antibodies, and hormones within the body, as well as serving as a transporter for vitamins, minerals, and fat in the blood. Last but not least, protein helps to maintain fluid balance both inside and out-

QUICK-GRAB PROTEIN
slices of lean meat (chicken, beef, pork)
milk
soy (powder, edamame, milk, etc.)
nut butter
almonds

side the cells. This is important because certain proteins in the blood regulate the balance of water in our tissues as we sweat. Without that mechanism, a person could run into serious issues with fluid loss, as well as electrolyte imbalances as a result of excessive sweat loss. That could then lead to muscle cramping, loss of coordination, or other serious medical issues.

Importance of protein for exercise:

// generates and repairs muscle tissue
// regulates water balance
// transports hormones, vitamins, minerals, and fat in blood
// manufactures enzymes

Protein is relied upon to a small extent during exercise, but its reparative abilities are the most important to you as a distance runner. And timing is everything. By consuming protein at the same time as carbohydrates following exercise, you minimize the damage done to the muscles and speed recovery. Most important, protein helps you as an athlete preserve lean muscle mass, which translates into better recovery and, therefore, higher-quality training. When lean muscle mass is protected and maintained, there is a greater opportunity for carbohydrates to be stored, further preserving lean muscle mass and leading to better fuel utilization during prolonged exercise. In extreme situations, that protein can be drawn upon as an energy source; however, it will come from the running muscles, signaling your body's slow breakdown. If you fuel the right way, fats and carbohydrates will provide the energy you need to successfully finish the half-marathon, and protein will be left to assist in post-run repair.

NUTRITION TAKEAWAYS

// There is no reason to shy away from carbohydrates, as long as the majority are complex.

// Fat is okay in moderation, especially the fats that come from seeds, nuts, and fish.

// Lean protein helps create and preserve muscle tissue and, if necessary, provides energy.

// Basically, eat a balanced diet, and you'll be well on your way to supporting optimal running performance.

Hydration: Staying ahead of the game

The human body is composed of two-thirds water, making hydration just as critical to a runner's performance as nutrition. The impact of even slight sweat loss on endurance performance may surprise you. Research has shown that even a 2 percent decrease in hydration stores, or a mere 3 pounds of sweat for a 150-pound runner, can negatively affect physical performance. Because sweat rates can reach up to 1–2 pounds per hour on a cool, dry day, imagine the loss in hot and humid conditions. The resulting physical response to dehydration is multi-faceted. Many of the effects stem from impaired cardiovascular functions via increased heart rate, decreased stroke volume, and decreased cardiac output. As discussed when we took a close look at physiology

sweat rate is the amount of sweat a person produces per hour. Most often, it is described in terms of pounds or ounces per hour.

in Chapter 2, all these affect a runner's VO_2max and, therefore, pace. Indeed, a 3 percent loss of sweat for that same 150-pound runner means a 4-8 percent decrease in aerobic capacity.

Besides the cardiac implications, dehydration leads to a number of other problems. First, it impairs your body's ability to dissipate heat, allowing your body temperature to rise. This not only will throw cold water on your performance but also will increase your risk of serious heat-related illnesses such as heat exhaustion and heatstroke. Gastrointestinal distress is another symptom, which may lead you to avoid drinking more fluids, making the problem even worse. Adding insult to injury, it can also cause an imbalance in electrolytes, which are critical for muscle contractions, leading to cramps, weakness, and incomplete conduction between nerves and muscles. Further, the decreased VO_2max will cause you to burn through your glycogen stores at a much higher rate. If this wasn't bad enough, dehydration can even result in cognitive impairment, meaning you may not even have the wits to pull over and stop running.

We aren't looking to scare you, but we do want to emphasize the importance of hydration. When determining the appropriate fluid intake, take into account the following factors that affect fluid loss:

HIGHER AMBIENT TEMPERATURES // Unsurprisingly, the hotter it is, the more you'll sweat.

HIGHER HUMIDITY // In certain cases, this can have a larger impact than actual air temperature. If it is warm or even hot, but not humid, your body can still cool itself. However, when it is humid, the mechanism that cools the body, sweating, doesn't work because the amount of moisture in the air is too high. Your sweat doesn't evaporate and create that cooling effect. Also, remember, the level of humidity close to your body can increase if you're wearing nonwicking materials next to the skin.

BODY SURFACE AREA // Bigger runners have a higher capacity to dissipate heat, but they also have increased surface area to gain heat, especially in hot weather. In essence, the bigger you are, the more likely you are to be hotter and sweat more.

CONDITION OF THE ATHLETE // A highly trained athlete has a much better cooling potential than a nonconditioned athlete. Although it may seem counterintuitive, a trained, heat-adapted runner will actually sweat more than a poorly conditioned runner. However, that conditioned athlete is better equipped to use this extra sweating to cool off more efficiently.

ORIGINAL STATE OF HYDRATION // If a runner is already slightly dehydrated going into an event, he or she will reach critical points of dehydration much sooner than an athlete who is well hydrated.

While it is important to understand how fluid is lost, you'll also want to know what factors impact fluid absorption. That is, after we ingest the fluid, how does it get from the stomach to the bloodstream, where we can actually use it? Let's start with carbohydrates. We already mentioned that they aid in the absorption of water; however, different types of carbs are absorbed at varying rates. Because carbohydrates are basically chains of molecules, the longer the chain, the more time it will take to exit the stomach. As scientists have begun to grasp the inner workings of this process, sports drink companies have started including two different lengths of chained carbohydrates in their beverages (usually dextrose and maltodextrin). With these drinks, you get the short chains that are quickly absorbed for immediate usage and the longer chains that assist in sustained absorption over time.

The amount of fluid you consume at any given time can also influence the rate of absorption. Although larger amounts of fluids ingested at one time are absorbed more quickly, for obvious reasons you aren't going to want to gulp down multiple cups of water at a single water stop during the race. Instead, start by consuming large amounts of fluids during the days leading up to the event and smaller quantities the day before and the morning of the race. Keep in mind that the temperature of the fluid can also increase or decrease absorption. At rest there appears to be no difference; during exercise, however, cooler fluids seem to leave the stomach much faster, while room-temperature drinks are more effectively utilized. Remember, the stomach is where food is primarily broken down, with actual absorption occurring in the small intestine.

Although you will have little control over the temperature of your drinks along the race course, you can influence other absorption-related factors, such as your relative state of hydration at the start line. Once you begin running, there is no turning back to correct your hydration status. If you're dehydrated at mile 1, you will continue to be dehydrated for the entire race. The progressive nature of dehydration makes it increasingly difficult to "catch up" once you're already at a deficit. Similarly, the faster you run, the harder it becomes for your body to absorb fluids into the bloodstream because the blood is pulled away from nonvital functions and directed toward the exercising muscles. Instead of circulating blood through the intestines and stomach, your system is working to pump blood to your legs to provide oxygen. Besides the physiological difficulties associated with absorbing fluids during fast running, there are also logistical challenges. Anyone who has ever tried to take a drink while running at 10K pace has probably experienced spilling more of the water than actually consuming it.

It is clear that monitoring your hydration status is as important to your half-marathon performance as any other aspect of training. Your hydration status will support you during easy runs, on SOS days, and in the race itself by keeping you healthy and allowing for consistent training. For the same reasons regular training is important, when it comes to mastering proper nutrition and hydration, practice makes perfect. It may take greater focus and attention in the beginning, but over time your judgment will improve and your base of fuel-related knowledge will expand.

While we spend a lot of time discussing fueling and hydration in relation to race day, these factors are equally important during training. Proper hydration takes a conscious effort every day; it is not achieved in a couple of hours before a workout but over a longer time. In the same way, carbohydrates need to be consumed and stored over the course of training to keep you running strong. Just like chronic carbohydrate depletion, chronic dehydration hinders performance. Similarly, protein will help with tissue repair between workouts, making each workout as productive as possible. So, even on the easy days, make a conscious effort to take in the proper fluids and fuel to replace what you have already utilized and prepare you for your next run.

HYPONATREMIA

Although a lot of media attention has focused on the relationship between long-distance running and hyponatremia in recent years, the topic remains murky. This condition occurs when there is an imbalance between the sodium and water contents in the blood. It tends to surface when a runner is losing a significant amount of sweat and simultaneously consuming large amounts of water. Because sodium is involved in nerve impulses and proper muscle function, this condition represents the disruption of an important balance within the body. There are three types of hyponatremia: euvolemic, when the water content increases and the sodium content stays the same; hypervolemic, when both the sodium and water contents increase, but the increase in water is far greater; and hypovolemic, when both sodium and water decrease, but sodium decreases faster. In all three instances, the concentration of sodium in the blood is diluted. It's like mixing a bottle of Gatorade, drinking half, and then refilling it with plain water, weakening the original mixture.

The effects of hyponatremia are very serious, as it can affect brain and muscle function to the point of coma and death. Despite these dangers, however, clear-cut guidelines for avoiding it are not readily available. In the end, remember that moderation in your hydration plan is important. Stick to the following guidelines:

// If your exercise session is more than an hour long, use a sports drink.
// Know your exercise sweat rate and consume liquids to that point. Although most people replace about 65–80 percent of their fluid losses, some people do drink beyond that point. (You can figure your sweat rate using the worksheet in Appendix B.)
// In recovery, focus on electrolyte-containing fluids. There are plenty of varieties that offer low-carbohydrate options for daily replacement.

What and when to eat and drink

PREWORKOUT

The hours before your workout can be the toughest time to dial in nutrition and hydration, especially for those trying to fit in early morning runs. While it would be ideal for you to get up an hour before your run to take in a bit of fuel, we understand that busy runners hold sleep in high regard. Every minute counts, for both running and sleeping. When considering your preworkout or pre-race routine, you have to weigh the pros and cons of time-related factors. If you have to cut your slumber to 5–6 hours just to get up and fuel an hour before your run, I say don't worry about it. You're better off grabbing a healthy snack before bed and getting more sleep. I always tell runners to address preworkout fueling on SOS days with particular focus because fuel depletion can compromise pace and performance. Easy days are less of a concern, since you won't need as much fuel to execute the workout. If you're running later in the day, however, you have a greater number of fueling options from which to choose. Typically, the more time you have, the more you should eat. As your workout approaches, the goal is to get in what you need the most of, namely, carbohydrates and fluids, without filling up too much. Table 8.2 outlines the basic guidelines for eating before workouts.

DURING WORKOUTS

A certain amount of trial and error is necessary as you fine-tune your overall fueling plan, but it is especially vital to test midrun nutrition during training. By getting this right, you'll avoid both dehydration and exhaustion of those precious carbohydrate stores. Because you'll be fueling throughout your half-marathon, practice drinking and refueling during workouts that exceed 1 hour. At times you may have to force yourself to eat and drink during a hard effort, but your body will thank

TABLE **8.2**	GUIDELINES FOR EATING BEFORE WORKOUTS	
TIME BEFORE WORKOUT	**OPTION**	**CONTENTS**
3–4 hours	meal	carbs, fat, protein
2 hours	snack	carbs, protein
1 hour	fluids	carbs
5–10 minutes	fluids or energy gel	carbs

you on race day. There is perhaps no greater performance booster than simple calories and hydration.

Hydration will undoubtedly give you the most bang for your buck in both training and racing. Not only will fluids help maintain blood volume levels, but sports drinks can provide crucial calories without your having to add another component to your plan. Your own sweat loss rate may vary, but on average, we lose between 2 and 4 pounds of sweat per hour during exercise. If that's not replaced, muscles receive less oxygen, less heat is evaporated, and by-products (lactic acid) accumulate in greater amounts. Among other outcomes, the body tries to compensate by making the heart beat faster. Indeed, for every 1 percent of body weight lost as a result of sweating, your heart rate will increase by up to 7 beats per minute. Furthermore, for every 1 percent of body weight lost through dehydration, you will slow down by about 2 percent. The race is already hard enough; the last thing you need is your heart thumping faster and your legs moving slower. At an 8:00-minute pace, a 2 percent loss in pace resulting from a 1 percent loss in body weight (as little as 1–2 pounds) translates into 5 lost seconds per mile. If you slow down by 2–4 percent, which is quite common, that 8:00-minute pace gets closer to an 8:20 pace. That is the difference between a 1:44 and a 1:49 half-marathon finish.

The most recent research (Butler et al., *Clin. J. Sports Med.*, 2006) says that when we drink based solely on thirst, somewhere between 68 and 82 percent of the lost fluid is recovered. These academicians suggest that the body compensates by basically pulling water from inside the cells to make up the difference, in addition to the natural formation of water through the combustion of fats and carbohydrates. While this undoubtedly occurs, they also discuss a major flaw in this line of thought. Their study indicated that all the aforementioned stipulations are true up to a 3 percent reduction in body weight caused by sweat loss. The problem is that if we do not drink until we are thirsty, we are already at about 2.3 percent (their calculation). Their subjects had unlimited access to fluid, but in reality you won't have the luxury of consuming 6–8 ounces whenever you feel like it. When I first read this study, I thought that perhaps everything we had been telling people was wrong. On further examination, however, I realized that our hydration strategies remain appropriate and pertinent in terms of real-world, endurance performance conditions. The following are the general hydration rules of thumb we recommend to runners. Those running less than 90 minutes may have less need for these guidelines, but those running 2 hours or more should certainly consider incorporating these guidelines into their training and racing.

START EARLY // Drink within the first 10–20 minutes of running or at the first water stop. As mentioned, thirst is a good indicator, but in the half-marathon scenario, you may not be able to physically get in very much fluid. It's hard to drink when you are flying!

DRINK 2–8 OUNCES OF FLUID EVERY 15–20 MINUTES // For training workouts, this means carrying sufficient water with you or placing it strategically beforehand. For races, this should work well with the water and sports drink stations. Most races provide these stations approximately every 2 miles.

// Keep in mind that it's easier to drink more during the early stages of a run or race. If you drink more early on and continue to replace fluids regularly, you will keep the stores topped off. This creates the fastest gastric emptying, which means more rapid absorption of water, electrolytes, and carbohydrates.

// Count the gulps. One gulp is roughly equal to 1 ounce of fluid. So, try for 4–6 gulps.

// Don't overdo it. Downing multiple cups of water will only make you sick.

PLAN AHEAD // If you are planning on using sports drinks (or gels) provided at the race, find out ahead of time what products will be offered and practice using the same ones in workouts. This will help you avoid unpleasant tummy troubles that can crop up when your system doesn't agree with a particular brand or type of product.

The guidelines for midrun nutrition are similar to those for hydration. Gels are probably the most popular refueling product, but other options, such as chews, are quickly gaining a following. Glucose tablets, which diabetics use to raise their blood sugar levels, are another alternative; they dissolve in your mouth and are a quick source of carbohydrates. Sports drinks will add precious calories to your overall intake, alleviating the need to consume as many calories from solid foods. Here's what we suggest:

CONSUME 30–60 GRAMS OF CARBOHYDRATE PER HOUR OF EXERCISE

// The longer you are out there, the more you should consume. For anything longer than 4 hours, take in 60 grams per hour.

// An 8-ounce sports drink supplies 50–80 calories.

// Gels provide 25 grams of carbohydrate.

TAKE IN 200–300 TOTAL CALORIES PER HOUR

// If you were to drink 8 ounces of sports beverage every 20 minutes, you would get roughly 195 calories per hour. This will be enough for most runners who are running less than 2 hours.

// In addition to fluids and gels, some runners choose to find calories elsewhere in other types of food. This all depends on what you prefer.

// If you use gels or something similar, chase with water, not a sports drink.

// One gel every 30–45 minutes should provide enough calories.

Beyond the clear physical support, a calculated fueling regimen can also play an important role in your mental game. My wife is a good example. She was running her first half-marathon since the birth of our daughter and wasn't feeling confident, as her training had been haphazard at best as we both adjusted to our new bundle of joy. Her plan was to carry a small handheld bottle with a gel in the pocket. I didn't think she needed any of it, but I didn't comment. At about 8 miles, she was looking spent, and I wondered how the rest of the race would play out. When I saw her at 10 miles, however, she looked revived and strong. She finished well and ran very even splits. The game changer for her? The gel. She said it woke her up and cleared the fog. The take-away point is this: She knew what she needed and had a plan. She took confidence in following that plan and saved herself from a potentially disheartening finish.

POSTWORKOUT

Refueling after a workout is just as important to the quality of your next workout as your preworkout nutrition was to the effort you just completed. This part of your nutrition plan is the easiest to carry out, so be sure not to overlook its significance. When all is said and done, proper postworkout fueling will help you recover from the run, maintain high levels of training, and ultimately become a better runner. We recommend the following plan for filling up after winding down:

THE INITIAL 15–30 MINUTES FOLLOWING EXERCISE ARE THE MOST IMPORTANT

// For every pound of body weight lost, replenish with 2.5 cups of water. To get an idea of how much water weight you tend to lose on a run, weigh yourself periodically throughout the first weeks of training, both before and after runs. With time you'll be able to make an educated guess about how much you should drink following a run. Check out the sweat loss calculator to learn your specific needs (see Appendix B).

// Immediately after your workout, take in 50–100 grams of carbohydrate. In particular, we recommend foods with a higher glycemic index because they will get into the bloodstream and be delivered to the muscles quickly. The glycemic index basically ranks foods on their rate of digestion. The quicker a food is digested, the higher the number. Try any of the following:

// bananas
// sports drinks
// oatmeal
// cooked carrots
// beans

// orange juice
// corn flakes
// baked potato
// bread
// ice cream

BEYOND THOSE FIRST 30 MINUTES AFTER EXERCISE, TRY TO EAT A MEAL WITHIN THE NEXT 2 HOURS // Oatmeal, peanut butter and a bagel, and cereal are great options, as is anything else that contains a large amount of healthy carbohydrates and some protein to promote muscle repair. A protein-rich drink, like chocolate milk, is a great option.

PLAN AHEAD // If you are driving to a group workout or to a park, pack something to consume when you are finished. Don't wait until you return home. Start the refueling process as soon as possible.

Fueling plan leading up to race day

Once all the hard work is done and you have cut back on both the volume and the intensity of your training, spend a little time fine-tuning your nutritional game plan. The following is a guide with tips for the final days leading up to the big race.

FINAL WEEK
// Although you have reduced your training volume, be sure to maintain a normal diet and avoid making any big changes.
// Seventy percent of your diet needs to be carbohydrates, primarily complex carbohydrates and starches. The increased

capacity for storage in your muscles will allow for the replenishment of all deficits. Research has shown that endurance can increase by as much as 20 percent through the complete restoration of glycogen stores.

// Gaining weight is a sign that you are doing things right, so don't worry if you tip the scales at an additional pound or so. Even gains of up to 5 pounds are common. While you may feel a bit sluggish, this is normal during the tapering period. Now is not the time to cut calories. Remember that every gram of stored carbohydrate is stored with 3 grams of water, and you'll need every bit of that on race day. That said, don't use this as an excuse to eat more. Rather, adjust your diet to your caloric needs.

// Hydrate throughout the week. Don't wait until the day prior to the race to play catch-up.

THE DAY BEFORE

// Drink a healthy beverage with every snack and meal. Rather than sticking with water, mix it up with sports drinks.

// Avoid foods that cause gas or gastrointestinal disruption.

// Avoid high-fiber foods.

// Avoid sugar substitutes.

// Limit alcohol.

// Eat or drink a healthy bedtime snack, such as unbuttered popcorn, a bagel and peanut butter, or a sports bar.

RACE MORNING

// The primary goal the few hours before the start of the race is to top off fuel stores and stay hydrated. For me that usually means a bagel and peanut butter, a banana, coffee, and maybe an orange juice about 3 hours before the race.

// Consume carbohydrates via these guidelines:

   1 hour prior: 50 grams total

   2 hours prior: 100 grams total

   3 hours prior: 150 grams total

   4 hours prior: 200 grams total

So, if you eat 4 hours out from the start of the race, your goal should be 200 grams of carbohydrates. If you eat 3 hours before the race, aim for 150 grams, and so on. Because most races begin fairly early in the morning, the majority of runners will be in the 2- to 3-hour window.

// The optimal amount of time to allow between eating and the start of the race varies based on the individual. Remember, if you eat early, you can always go back to bed. If you have a sensitive stomach, a substantial bedtime snack may be preferable.

// Balance topping off reserves with having to stand in long lines for the bathroom. If you come into race day well fueled, you won't have to worry about any last-minute fueling measures.

Race fueling strategy

When it comes to the full marathon distance, I can't stress enough the importance of nutrition during the race. However, for the half-marathon, much depends on an individual runner's finish time. For runners who will finish in under 90 minutes, being well fueled and hydrated leading up to the race is probably all they need to worry about. For runners who will finish in 2 or more hours, having an appropriate fueling strategy to execute during the race could mean the difference between an impressive personal best and not even being able to reach the finish line. With race nutrition and hydration, for any runner regardless of finishing time, your two main goals should be to minimize extreme fluid loss and maintain glycogen levels (as mentioned, faster runners who start with a full tank may be fine without fueling during the race).

In figuring out how and what you should consume, several factors should be considered. First, caloric expenditure is more closely aligned with the distance traveled rather than with the pace. Although a faster runner is exercising at a higher intensity, he or she will burn about the same number of calories as a slower runner of the same weight. However, while pace might not matter, weight does. Put simply, for every kilogram of body weight, we burn 1 calorie for every kilometer we run (1 cal/kg/km). Because it's easy to check how much you weigh (to convert to kilograms, divide your weight in pounds by 2.2), and we know the distance of a half-marathon (21.0975 km), we can easily calculate how many calories you will burn during the race.

Example: 150-lb. runner

150 lb. ÷ 2.2 kg/lb. = 68.18 kg

cal. burned = 21.0975 × 68.18 = 1,438 cal.

Those 1,438 calories will be a mixture of fat and carbohydrate calories. To figure out the ratio, you must consider how fast you will be traveling, because the faster you run, the more carbohydrates you use. Typical half-marathon pace is usually around 60 percent of VO_2max for beginners, 75 percent for advanced runners, and 85 percent for elite runners. This information is enough to give us a general idea of what ratio of carbohydrate to fat will result. See Table 8.3 for the appropriate mix of carbohydrate and fat calories at various running intensities.

TABLE 8.3	CARBOHYDRATE AND FAT PERCENTAGES FOR VARIOUS RUNNING INTENSITIES	
VO₂MAX	CARBOHYDRATE	FAT
65%	60%	40%
75%	70%	30%
85%	80%	20%

The next step involves figuring out how many calories per mile (or kilometer) are being used. Consider the previous example of the runner who will expend 1,438 calories during the race. To figure out expenditure per mile, simply divide 1,438 by 13.1. The result is roughly 110 calories per mile. From here we can calculate the range of carbohydrate expenditure per mile. At 60 percent, the ratio would be 110 × 0.60, or 66 calories of carbohydrate per mile. At 75 percent, the ratio would be 110 × 0.7, or 77 calories per mile. Finally, at 85 percent, the carbohydrate expenditure would be 93.5 calories per mile. Given these values and depending on the pace the runner is attempting, the total caloric expenditure from carbohydrate would look like this:

cal./mile (66, 77, and 93.5) × 13.1 miles or
a range of 864.6–1,224.85 cal.

This difference amounts to about 350 calories, which may not seem like much, but it actually equals about three extra energy gels (100 calories each). This also shows how imperative it is to run at an appropriate intensity during the race. Even a few seconds faster per mile for a significant amount of time could put you at a carbohydrate deficit from which you might not be able to recover. While we want you to set your sights high and race to the best of your abilities, some risks aren't worth taking.

Although we have calculated a range of necessary carbohydrates, we still haven't discussed how many you should actually replace, which largely depends on the amount that is stored in your exercising muscles. Although the liver also stores glycogen, it would prefer to reserve it for the brain and central nervous system, so it's best if you can leave those stores alone. While trained athletes store about 80 calories per gram in their muscles, that glycogen is available only for local use. In other words, glycogen in your arms won't be available for use in your legs. On average, leg mass constitutes approximately 21 percent of total mass in males and 20 percent in females. With this information, we can figure out our potential carbohydrate storage. To calculate your needs, take your weight in kilograms and multiply it by 20 or 21 percent to calculate leg mass. From there, multiply by 80 cal./kg to determine your average glycogen storage. Tables 8.4 and 8.5 show the potential carbohydrate storage for males and females at various weights.

68.18 kg × 0.21 = 14.32 kg

14.32 kg × (80 cal./kg) = 1,146 cal. of potential carbohydrate storage (for running use)

Given our 68.18-kg example, we found that this runner can store 1,146 calories for use while running. We also know that this runner will expend 864–1,224 calories over the course of the entire race. If he's running at 75–85 percent VO_2max, which wouldn't be unusual, then he's going to need a little bit of help by way of extra calories during the race. Getting this right is the trick with the half-marathon for many

TABLE 8.4	POTENTIAL CARBOHYDRATE STORAGE FOR MALES	
VO$_2$MAX	CARBOHYDRATE	FAT
65 kg (143 lb.)	14 kg	1,092 cal.
70 kg (154 lb.)	15 kg	1,176 cal.
75 kg (165 lb.)	16 kg	1,260 cal.
80 kg (176 lb.)	17 kg	1,344 cal.
85 kg (187 lb.)	18 kg	1,428 cal.
90 kg (198 lb.)	19 kg	1,512 cal.
95 kg (209 lb.)	20 kg	1,596 cal.
100 kg (220 lb.)	21 kg	1,680 cal.
110 kg (242 lb.)	23 kg	1,848 cal.
120 kg (264 lb.)	25 kg	2,016 cal.

Potential carbohydrate storage in leg muscles for males gives an average 21 percent of total mass.

recreational runners. There is a chance you can make it all the way—or that it could all come to a screeching halt. Following the guidelines we have provided, this runner can develop a comprehensive plan to optimize fuel storage potential and maintain energy throughout the race. Remember that this replacement plan will get you to the finish line, but there is no way to keep the tank completely full. The nutrition aspect of half-marathon training and racing is about optimizing those stores by teaching your body to burn fat more efficiently.

As with most dietary guidelines and recommendations, these numbers are based on averages. A runner who is extremely fit, lean, and

TABLE 8.5	POTENTIAL CARBOHYDRATE STORAGE FOR FEMALES	
VO$_2$MAX	CARBOHYDRATE	FAT
45 kg (99 lb.)	9 kg	720 cal.
50 kg (110 lb.)	10 kg	800 cal.
55 kg (121 lb.)	11 kg	880 cal.
60 kg (132 lb.)	12 kg	960 cal.
65 kg (143 lb.)	13 kg	1,040 cal.
70 kg (154 lb.)	14 kg	1,120 cal.
75 kg (165 lb.)	15 kg	1,200 cal.
80 kg (176 lb.)	16 kg	1,280 cal.
85 kg (187 lb.)	17 kg	1,360 cal.
90 kg (198 lb.)	18 kg	1,440 cal.

Potential carbohydrate storage in leg muscles for females gives an average 20 percent of total mass.

muscular, with a high proportion of slow-twitch muscle fibers, may have higher storage capabilities. Regardless of these factors, all runners should err on the side of caution. If your stomach can tolerate the calories, there is no reason not to consume them. We can't emphasize enough the importance of nutritional dress rehearsals before race day. You should toe the line knowing exactly when and what you'll be eating and drinking the entire 13.1 miles.

9

Gearing up

MY COLLEGE TRACK COACH always used to say, "You can't run fast if you don't look good!" While he may have simply been referring to our shirts not being tucked in, it does beg the question of whether or not our shoes and apparel really make a notable difference in our performance. Certainly for the sake of comfort, certain running-specific items are now a necessity, such as quality running shoes. As one with 75,000-plus miles on my legs, I can make a compelling personal case for shoes keeping a career going. However, there remains a lot of debate out there on the topic—and a lot of choice. One thing is for sure: We've come a long way from Emil Zatopek running repeats through the woods in his combat boots!

Shoes are an extension of your personal biomechanics. While there are a lucky few who have textbook bones and musculature, chances are you don't. Most runners have at least a couple of minor imperfections that predispose them to injury, like one leg that's a little longer than the other, a fallen arch, or a weak pelvis. This is where shoes come into play.

Getting fitted in the right pair of shoes is as important as training smart and eating right. To help you with the shoe selection process, we will discuss stride biomechanics, foot type, and the various components to look for in a shoe. For the minimalists out there, I'll dabble in that debate, as well. I'll also mention some principles for choosing among the colorful displays of apparel that you will find. After reading this chapter, you should be ready to go to your local running specialty store, confer with an expert, and choose the best shoes and apparel for you.

Running stride biomechanics

When it comes to selecting the right shoe, several factors must be considered. One is the point of impact between the foot and the ground, referred to as the foot strike. A related consideration is how long your foot stays on the ground during each step. With foot strike, the goal is to be brief enough that braking forces (which slow you down and are jarring to your body) are minimized, but not so brief that the maximal force used to move the body forward is compromised. It may not seem like foot strike could have a significant overall impact on performance, but in the long term, it makes a big difference. Consider this: Over the course of 5 kilometers, a runner finishing in 30 minutes will take a whopping 5,400 steps. By decreasing foot strike time by just 1/100 of a second, he or she would run a whole minute faster over 5 kilometers. Extrapolate that to the half-marathon, and you're talking about potentially shaving minutes off your time, merely by striking more efficiently.

Though there are certain universal truths concerning foot strike biomechanics, much debate over the ideal place to land still exists, questioning whether the heel, midfoot, or forefoot is best. Studies examining this aspect of running should be read with caution. For every study that comes out saying one thing, another study draws a different conclusion. This area of examination is clearly still open for debate. However, the more information that comes out, the more it appears that foot strike is highly individual to our own biomechanics. One of the more reliable studies, published in the *Journal of Strength and Conditioning Research* in 2007 (Hasegawa et al., "Footstrike Patters of Runners at the 15-km Point During an Elite-Level Half Marathon," 21[3]: 888–893), looked at the foot strike patterns of elite runners during a half-marathon race. The results showed that nearly 75 percent of them landed on their heels, while 24 percent landed midfoot, and just 1 percent were forefoot strikers. It should also be noted that 60 percent of the first 50 finishers of the race were midfoot strikers.

Because the research is somewhat unreliable in even categorizing the various types of foot strike, it is more productive to look at the matter in a different way. What I have noticed both anecdotally while working with runners and by studying the emerging research is that where the foot lands, relative to your body weight, is probably more important than what part of the foot is landing. For instance, landing on the heel first isn't necessarily bad, provided the foot is landing close to a runner's center of gravity (in other words, underneath him). But if the same runner is landing heel first and his foot is far out in front, then he is overstriding—an underlying cause of many issues and injuries—and probably could benefit from a form fix or a different shoe.

One reason runners overstride is in an attempt to cover more distance with each stride. However, the action is counterproductive because it creates a braking motion and forces your legs to absorb more shock. What happens when people try to lengthen their stride is they just try to throw their leg farther out in front of them. By doing that, they land with their foot way too far in front of their body and land directly on their heel and with their toes way up in the air. This increases the time they are in contact with the ground, and as a consequence their pace also slows. If you focus on landing beneath your center of gravity, you'll avoid these issues.

While the verdict is still out in the academic world, we recommend simply proceeding with training and not becoming too preoccupied with altering your natural form. There are, however, a couple of practical tips concerning foot strike that may help you run more efficiently. First, as we just suggested, avoid overstriding. Instead of trying to develop monster strides, think about lifting your legs with the quads and pulling the lower leg underneath the quad upon each strike with the ground. This will cause you to land under your center of gravity and on the middle of your foot. The other variable that you can tinker with to develop a more efficient foot strike is posture. When you hear a coach tell a runner to "run tall," that means keeping the shoulders pulled back, with a slight bend at the waist; avoid slouching your shoulders, and view your entire torso up to your head as a single lever. The slight forward lean will keep you from overdoing posture and ending up looking like a drum major in a marching band. Remember, your pelvis should be beneath your center of gravity, and your feet striking under you, with neither out in front of your body.

Foot type

In addition to the way you strike the ground with each step, the actual shape of your feet should play a role in your shoe selection process. Among the many shapes and sizes of human beings, three major foot types come to the forefront: those with flat arches, high arches, and medium arches. Through coaching and working at the Hansons Running Shops, we have found that the flat foot, although not the most common, is definitely the most troublesome. In addition to having a flatter arch, flat feet are often accompanied by ankles that lean inward toward one another. When running, individuals with this foot type tend to land on the outsides of their feet, and as they proceed through the foot strike, the foot and ankle roll inward, also referred to as overpronation. Some amount of pronation is normal as the foot naturally rolls inward, providing shock attenuation and giving the body leverage to push off from the ground, but a flat-footed runner who overpronates, or rolls inward too much, tends to experience an increase in certain overuse injuries. The main problem is that this runner's feet tend to be too flexible, cushioning the blow of the foot slamming into the ground but also providing little leverage to carry the body through the striking motion to assist in pushing off from that step. This excessive motion leads to a host of rotational forces applied to the foot, ankle, shin, and knee, creating issues like tendinitis, plantar fasciitis, and Achilles tendinitis. As you may have guessed, this foot type requires a very specific shoe to alleviate these problems and allow for normal running.

The second type of foot is one that has a high arch, which is, unsurprisingly, the exact opposite of the flat foot. A runner with this foot type also lands on the outside of the foot but remains there all the way through toe-off (the point at which the toes propel the runner forward as the foot is pushed off from the ground). While the flat foot offers great natural cushioning but is a poor lever for pushing off, the reverse is true for the high-arched foot. Along with high arches comes inflexibility, so the feet are unable to do a good job of absorbing the forces that running imposes on the body. All the weight is put on the outside of the foot during ground contact; as a result, even the toe-off is somewhat limited because it can't take full advantage of the big toe to push off. Ironically, this motion, called underpronation or supination, can lead to some of the same injuries as overpronation but for different reasons. While rotational forces tend to be the cause of injuries in flat-footed runners, poor shock absorption is the plight of supinators. In addition, this foot type may lead to a greater number of issues with the iliotibial band, the long band of tissue that stretches from the pelvis down to the knee joint.

The third foot type is somewhere in the middle, with a medium (neutral) arch. Although it is often labeled as "normal," that is not to say it is the most common. In fact, it is the least common. The lucky runner with this foot type will have a foot strike that likely begins at the middle to the outside of the heel and then gently rolls to the middle of the foot, continuing to use the leverage of the big toe, therefore maximizing toe-off. Although the biomechanics may be better, a medium-arched runner still runs the risk of injury by running in a shoe that is too supportive or not supportive enough. As we have alluded, each biomechanical difference comes with its own set of unique challenges, making it particularly important to choose a shoe that is made for your arch type. For a completely accurate assessment of your foot type and accompanying shoe category, seek out advice from a professional at a running specialty store or from a gait analysis expert. You can do tests at home to determine your foot type, such as a simple wet test, but they don't always guarantee a proper shoe prescription. The wet test is simply stepping on a dry towel with your wet feet. The impression that your foot leaves will give you an indiciation of your arch height or type. When choosing a shoe, it is important not only to consider your foot type but also to understand the motion of your feet when running, as well as other biomechanical issues.

Remember that we all have physiological imperfections. Being biomechanically, anatomically, and genetically blessed is a rarity, even at the elite level. I recently saw a picture that featured several elite American 10K runners. It showed their 10K times and photos of their footstrikes. I didn't see one that would be considered biomechanically perfect. So the real question is whether what you are currently doing is keeping you healthy and running pain free. If not, you must decide whether or not you can address the issue with an appropriate shoe.

Shoe construction

To understand what type of shoe may be best for your feet, you should be familiar with the various components that make up running-specific footwear. The main pieces are the outsole, midsole, last, heel counter, and upper.

THE OUTSOLE

Let's start at the bottom with the outsole of a shoe, also known as the tread. Until recently, the outsole did little more than provide traction, with the only variation existing in the type of rubber used. Now, however, there are a growing number of technologies used for outsoles. Instead of one piece of rubber, the outsoles are often broken into pods for the heel and forefoot, which saves weight. Also, rather than rubber, today's companies are relying on new materials, like silica, which are said to provide better traction in wet conditions, as well as being more environmentally friendly. Outsole technology has also improved in terms of the general wear of the shoe, meaning you can get more miles out of a pair of shoes. In fact, for most runners, the midsole breaks down well before the outsole.

THE MIDSOLE

The midsole is where most of the action occurs from a biomechanical standpoint. In recent years, once-popular midsole materials, like ethyl vinyl acetate (EVA) and air pockets, have been replaced with new technologies that are more resilient, lighter, and biodegradable. Cushioning technology has also improved, allowing the shoes to absorb forces more readily and last up to 15 percent longer.

While all midsoles contain cushioning, the amount of support varies. Depending on how much stability a runner needs, some shoes contain a denser midsole to provide more support, including dual-density and tri-density materials. This type of midsole helps to keep an overpronating foot in a more neutral position, but it also adds weight to the shoe. Different shoe models contain varying amounts of these materials, leading to a wide variety of stability and weight options. To spot a shoe that contains a denser midsole, look for a gray area that constitutes part of the medial side (inside) of the midsole. Other pieces are sometimes added for extra support, such as roll bars, which make for an even stiffer shoe. The more a person pronates, the more he or she will need these extra components.

When you buy a good pair of running shoes, the midsole is where your money is going. Instead of looking at the tread to determine whether your shoes need to be replaced, it is more important to consider the number of miles you've run in the shoe and the wear and tear on the midsole (average life expectancy is 300–500 miles). Despite all the technological advances, shoes still break down, and as soon as the midsole is past its prime, you're at risk for injury.

THE LAST

The last is the actual shape of the shoe. There are three basic lasts: straight, curved, and semicurved. Each of these varieties is correlated with a different foot type to control motion optimally. For instance, a straight last is the best foundation for an overpronating runner because it helps control the excessive inward rolling that characterizes the motion of a flat-footed runner, also providing for better toe-off. The curved last offers the opposite of the straight last; instead of being symmetrical, it is markedly curved along the medial side of the shoe where the arch sits. A curved last is built for supinators to help deal with the poor natural cushioning by promoting a slight inward roll. Finally, the semicurved last can be considered a hybrid between the curved and straight varieties; it is tailored to runners with a medium (neutral) arch, allowing for natural pronation.

THE HEEL COUNTER

You can't see the heel counter, which is a unit that hugs the heel to minimize motion in the ankle. Because some runners need this type of control and others don't, there are varying levels of heel counter stability, with the most flexible shoes having no heel counter at all.

THE UPPER

The lightweight material that covers the top of the foot is known as the upper. Usually made of a highly breathable nylon mesh, the upper permits sweat and water to be wicked away from the feet, keeping them cool and dry. If you live in a cold-weather state, there are uppers that provide more weather-resistant capabilities to keep snow and slush out of the shoe. You'll also notice the various lacing patterns of different uppers; many of the newest versions help to hug the arch and provide a bit of extra support.

Shoe type

Despite the seemingly endless array of options, running shoes fall into specific categories. Just as there are three foot types, there are three main classes of shoes. Even so, there are many shades of gray, recently making way for a fourth, and perhaps a fifth, category. We will discuss the following shoe types: motion control, neutral, stability, lightweight, and minimalist.

MOTION CONTROL

This shoe is designed for the flattest of feet. A typical motion-control shoe is built atop a straight last and has a dual-density midsole from the heel to beyond the arch, a plastic roll bar in the heel and arch, and a stiff heel counter. With all the extras, these shoes aren't your lightest option, but they are good at their main job, which is to prevent overpronation.

NEUTRAL

These shoes are best suited for a runner who has high arches. They are built on a curved last with loads of cushioning, no dual-density midsole materials, and a minimal heel counter. The goal of this type of footwear is to provide cushioning and flexibility without tipping the scales.

STABILITY

The stability category is for neutral and mildly overpronating "normal" runners. The last is typically semicurved, with some dual-density midsole technology, a flexible forefoot, ample cushioning, and a mild heel counter. This type of shoe provides a nice middle-of-the-road option for a runner who needs a slight amount of support without sacrificing cushioning.

LIGHTWEIGHT

While lightweight shoes have been around for a long time, they are becoming increasingly mainstream, falling somewhere between a regular running shoe and a racing flat. They are akin to a lightweight version of a neutral shoe, with certain exceptions that include supportive features. For most runners, they shouldn't be worn exclusively in training. From a practical standpoint, they just won't last very long. Lightweight means less material, which translates into decreased durability, support, and cushioning. For these reasons, the average runner will likely prefer a more substantial shoe. Lightweight shoes are, however, a good option for certain runners to wear for specific SOS workouts, especially speed and strength work. Racing flats are a subcategory of lightweight shoes. For the same reasons already stated, they should be used only in certain circumstances, like racing! They tend to have even less material and have a life expectancy of about 100–150 miles.

MINIMALIST

Because minimalist footwear has opened the floodgates to much controversy, it is worth spending a little time explaining the debate so you can decide if you want to try a shoe from this fast-growing category. Minimalist footwear offers little if any cushioning or true protection for the feet, allowing you to feel as if you're running barefoot. While this type of footwear has gained plenty of notoriety in recent years, the recommendations on wearing minimalist shoes have aroused much argument. From Olympic coaches to weekend warriors, it seems that everyone has an opinion. Initially, the Hansons wouldn't sell the trend-driven minimalist models, not so much because they thought the shoes were simply a fad but mainly because people just aren't very good at following directions. Consumers wanted these shoes because they were light, fashionable, and the new cool thing. Although the box usually gives specific instructions to begin using the shoes very gradually, people would lace them up and head out for 5 miles right off the bat. After a week of running in the minimalist shoes, they'd end up injured without understanding why.

Today it is impossible to ignore the minimalist movement, and most running specialty stores, including Hansons Running Shops, stock at least a couple of models. To help you decide if such a shoe is right for you, let's take a serious look at the origins as well as the pros and cons of minimalism. First, it is important to understand the premise of minimalism, which includes two basic ideas: (1) You should wear the least amount of shoe that you can tolerate without getting hurt, and (2) by wearing less shoe, you strengthen the feet and improve your running stride. Minimalist advocates often argue that our ancestors were made to run barefoot, so we should get back to basics and do the same. The key word here is "ancestors." These folks didn't wear shoes for 20 years and then decide to go run barefoot for a 10-miler. Living in a world much different from that of our Paleolithic forefathers and foremothers, we wear shoes from the time we are very young, so a transition from wearing shoes to going barefoot is necessary. Most proponents of minimalism suggest taking a gradual approach to decreasing the amount of shoe over the course of several months. If you are wearing a stability model, for instance, you should not go directly to a minimalist shoe but perhaps transition with a lightweight trainer before moving to the minimalist or "barefoot" footwear. This allows the bones and soft tissues to gradually adjust to the minimalist footwear. Even after you have fully transitioned, we don't recommend wearing this type of shoe every day for regular training; instead, think of it as a training supplement to be worn periodically.

Another argument supplied by the minimalist movement states that running in less of a shoe helps strengthen your feet. While not many will argue against this notion, the idea should be approached with prudence. For those of you who have run in racing flats or track spikes, or even done speed work, think about how sore your calves are the following day. Running in minimalist shoes elicits similar strain and resulting fatigue and soreness. Now imagine that you place this same stress on the calves day after day by continuing to wear this type of footwear. How long would you guess it would take before injuries arise? The current research says about two weeks (Lieberman et al., "Foot Strike Patterns and Collision Forces in Habitually Barefoot Versus Shod Runners," *Nature* 463 [January 28, 2010]: 531–535). The point is that most people don't take the time to safely transition from regular shoes to minimalist footwear, causing a seemingly endless list of problems.

The final contention made by minimalist supporters is that wearing less of a shoe will improve running form, the goal being to encourage forefoot or midfoot striking over heel striking. The basic thought is that landing on the midfoot reduces impact forces, diminishing not only the risk of injury but also the need for shoe cushioning. Studies have shown that barefoot runners who land on the forefoot display significantly lower impact forces than runners who wear shoes and land on their heels. This information is certainly interesting; nevertheless, the available research on the subject is limited, making it important to dissect each new study. The primary findings of current research are that runners who are accustomed to running barefoot or in minimalist shoes usually land on the midfoot and forefoot. They also tend to land with significantly lower impact force than a runner wearing shoes. On the other hand, runners who aren't adapted to running barefoot or in minimalist footwear will most likely land on their heels when they take off their shoes. The result of this is a landing force that is nearly seven times greater than when landing on the heel while wearing shoes. For many runners, it's best to stick with their normal shoes (ibid.).

One of the main arguments against wearing shoes is that they don't reduce the risk of injury. It is true that the injury rate of runners has hovered around 70 percent for the last four decades. However, the statistics potentially offer alternate explanations that don't involve the issue of footwear. According to Running USA, the number of half-marathon finishers went from 612,000 people in 2004 to more than 1.6 million in 2011! Along with that, given the general trends in obesity, one could assume that the weight of the average endurance runner has also increased. Simply put, a far wider range of the overall population spectrum is running half-marathons than ever before, which means that more injuries are bound to happen. It is safe to postulate that, perhaps, traditional running shoes and the new technologies introduced over the years have actually helped keep more runners healthy, rather than the opposite. There is simply no way of knowing with certainty, but this is what many coaches believe.

In deciding what is best for you as a runner, consider the research along with your own biomechanics and injury history. Minimalist running will work for some, but not for others. If you want to try it, be patient and allow yourself a considerable amount of time to make the transition, especially if you are running high mileage. Using this footwear will require a significant reduction in your training, so experimenting with it at the beginning of a training cycle isn't a good idea. Our suggestion is first to wear something like a lightweight trainer for SOS workouts (other than long runs) and regular trainers the other days to see how your body responds. As always, pay attention to what your body is telling you, read the research for yourself, and ignore ostentatious claims made by the media.

Footwear pricing

One of the most common questions runners ask about shoes relates to price. Indeed, not all shoes are created equal. As in buying a car, the more features you want or need, the more you're going to pay. Remember, however, that shoe type, not cost, should guide your decision; the most expensive shoe is not necessarily the best one for you. When you head to the store, be sure to consider your specific needs and make an informed decision. There are three basic price points: entry-level, midgrade, and high-end.

ENTRY-LEVEL

Your cheapest option, these shoes offer the basics but not much else. They are great for someone just getting into the sport, especially those who aren't even sure they'll continue running. Most entry-level shoes are made with cushioning in the heel but not in the forefoot. They are noticeably less responsive and just don't feel as comfortable as high-end models. Even so, these shoes are reliable and well constructed, and they get the job done. They will also be the cheapest way to get out of a running shop. While even less expensive running shoes can be found at department stores, we never recommend choosing anything below this category.

MIDGRADE

The most popular price point among running shoes, models that fall into this category offer the basics, plus a few extras like full-length cushioning, better midsole material, a more responsive feel, and an enhanced overall fit. A blend of luxury and functionality, this category of shoe will be able to withstand a few more miles than the entry-level shoes.

HIGH-END

Shoes in this category have all the bells and whistles in terms of the latest technology, whether you need them or not, and are often a company's "premier" model. You may get a little more wear out of these shoes, but runners need to weigh whether the higher price tag is worth it for their individual needs.

How to choose a shoe

With a firm understanding of the various types of running shoes on the market, you are now ready to move forward with selecting a pair that is right for you. The most important step you can take is to go to a running specialty store rather than making a purchase at an online superstore. While some get lucky selecting shoes off the Internet, you are far more likely to get the right fit if you have a knowledgeable employee assist you with the fitting process. Selecting the right shoes is like putting together the pieces of a puzzle; a well-trained employee will help you find the missing pieces and make a good choice. When you go to the store, be sure to bring along your old running shoes and come ready to answer questions about your training and past running experience, such as:

// "Have you had any injuries?"
// "How did you last shoes treat you?"
// "Have you been fitted for running shoes before?"

Next, a running shop specialist is likely to examine the wear pattern on the bottom of your old shoes to get a general idea of how you strike the ground. For instance, if you tend to grind down the entire medial (inside) side of the tread, you're most likely overpronating and need more support than that shoe offers. Conversely, if the outside edge is worn, you're probably supinating and need less support and more cushioning. If your wear pattern is even, you're likely already in the correct shoe category. It is important to keep in mind that this isn't an exact science. If you've gone through 10 versions of the same model and haven't had any issues with injuries, stick with what you know works for you, regardless of wear pattern.

In most running specialty shops, the employee will also ask to observe your gait. Many running establishments have treadmills and cameras that capture images of the motion of your feet during walking and running. When the images are slowed down on the screen, you can see exactly how you are striking. Even without such technology, an experienced employee can watch you walk or run and get a good idea of what type of shoe you should wear. If you're looking to go a step beyond, you can visit a sports performance lab and get a gait analysis with the use of special software for a reasonable fee. Another new technology that is becoming more popular is a basic force pad that the runner stands on without shoes. This force, or pressure, pad shows the outline of the foot and gives a fairly accurate idea of arch type. It also shows where you place the most pressure, which can help determine where you might need more cushioning and whether you need any stability in the shoes. You also usually receive a printout of your foot scan, along with recommendations on shoe type.

Once you are presented with several options of shoes that are appropriate for your feet, the responsibility is on you to decide which pair is the most comfortable. Be sure to select the right size; just because your dress shoes are a size 9, don't assume your running shoes will be the same. When you put the shoes on, consider these factors:

HEEL // The heel should provide a snug fit, preventing any slippage.

TOE BOX // There should be a bit of room in the toe box in terms of both length and width. Your toes should have room to splay out and push off when you're running, but you don't want so much room that your feet slide around.

TIMING // If you can arrange it, go to the store around the same time of day you'd normally run, because your feet swell throughout the day. What feels like the right size in the morning can be too tight after a day spent on your feet.

The final decision usually comes down to how the shoe fits your feet. When given three shoes from the same category and price range, it is likely any of them will do the job. Choose the one that feels the best. Remember to select your shoes based on function, not fashion. By understanding foot types and shoe categories, and by working with a knowledgeable employee at a running specialty store, you'll end up with a pair of shoes that will serve you well during your training.

When to replace shoes

We have found that most runners who are new to our training programs assume they can purchase a new pair of shoes at the beginning of training and wear them all the way through race day. The flaw in this reasoning is made apparent when the runner realizes that a pair of shoes can carry a person for only 300–500 miles, depending on the shoe, body type, and running style. The Beginner Program has you running a total of about 640 miles over 18 weeks of training, putting anyone who uses that plan well beyond the expiration date. In reality, you will need two pairs to get you through training and the race itself. While a lucky few may be able to make it through training without swapping out their shoes, the large majority of runners will find new injuries pop up as their shoes age. It may be your shins, your knees, or the bottoms of your feet because, when a shoe breaks down, you lose the intended support and cushioning. Without those features, you expose yourself to the common injuries that occur with your particular foot type.

In most cases, we suggest getting fit for one pair, trying them out for a few weeks, and then deciding whether to purchase an identical pair or a different model. If you end up loving the first pair you bought, make sure that the model hasn't changed when you go to buy the next pair. Although the name may be the same, models can differ from one season to the next, bringing along significant issues with fit that may not jibe with your preferences and overall comfort.

Race day kicks

Your first run in a new pair of shoes most certainly should not be on race day, advice that is echoed in every running shop and by every coach across the country. Most shoes are ready to be worn right out of the box, requiring little to no break-in time, but it is important to make sure that the specific pair of shoes you'll be wearing for your 13.1-mile race will be comfortable. While you could wear multiple pairs of the same model with no problems, you still need to give your body time to adjust to the new shoe. If you think about it, it makes perfect sense. As a shoe slowly breaks down, your foot adjusts to its slightly changing makeup. However, when you lace up that brand-new pair right off the store shelves, your feet have to make an immediate adjustment to the more substantial thickness of the midsole and the shape of the upper. This goes for runners who wear orthotics too. Just as your feet need to adapt to the new shoe, so do your inserts. The shoes you race in should have enough mileage to feel familiar, but not so many miles that they are beginning to break down. For most runners, this falls between 50 and 100 miles, meaning two to three weeks before the race.

When selecting a race day shoe, most runners will choose a model in which they can also log plenty of training miles, although some runners look for a lighter shoe for race day. When deciding whether or not to lighten up for the big day, consider that you're going to be on your feet for a long time, longer than for any of your training runs. That means your feet are going to swell and may be in need of a slightly bulkier shoe that has adequate cushioning to take the brunt of the force upon each foot strike. Keep in mind that racing flats are lighter because they lack cushioning and support. Because fatigue will have a detrimental effect on running mechanics and running economy, you become more susceptible to injury as you tire. We ask most runners considering flats, "Why sacrifice a couple of ounces that may ultimately take a toll on your biomechanics?"

So when is a good time to wear flats? The more competitive you are, the more you should consider wearing flats. If you already do your SOS days in a lightweight trainer, minimalist shoe, or racing flat, then you could certainly entertain the idea of wearing a flat on race day. When it comes to making this decision, however, recognize that you will be trading the comfort and security of cushioning and stability for a lighter weight. Some runners really need that extra cushioning and support, especially during the later stages of the race. If you are in this camp but are still interested in going lighter, consider the lightweight trainer category. In recent years these types of shoes have emerged as a great transitional option between a regular training shoe and a racing flat. They aren't as substantial as your everyday training shoe, but they will offer enough support and cushioning for limited use, like a half-marathon. This would allow you to save a couple of ounces of shoe weight without running the risk of injury.

In my experience, I have found that running in regular training shoes works for most of my daily runs. However, for the long runs when I'm looking to pick up the pace, I often choose lighter-weight, more flexible shoes that still support my low arches. It isn't much, but that decreased weight makes me feel faster, while the shoes still offer the protection I need to keep me from getting injured, especially because I wear them only for certain workouts. If you decide to purchase a second pair of lightweight trainers, be sure to wear them for a few workouts before racing in them so you will know whether they will work for the big day.

Apparel

While apparel and accessories are also important to half-marathon training, this is simply too vast a category for the focus of this book. What you wear on race day will depend on both weather and what you have worn in training. For instance, a running cap may be a perfect accessory for a rainy, cool race in March; in July, it may do nothing but trap heat. The following are some basic guidelines to keep in mind when choosing your ensemble:

AVOID COTTON // Don't wear any cotton socks, shorts, pants, or shirts. Instead of helping to wick moisture and heat away from your body, cotton traps heat and absorbs sweat, creating a humid environment close to your skin. This can lead to both chafing and blisters.

DRESS DOWN // Pretend it's 20 degrees warmer than it actually is when choosing your outfit. If it's 40 degrees outside, dress like it is 60. You will be chilly the first mile, but once you start generating heat, you will warm up quickly.

CONSIDER COST // Consider cost per wear when purchasing running clothing. It's not about the initial investment, but rather how much wear you are going to get out of it. Good running apparel can be pricey, but it is quite durable and should last several seasons.

TRY IT ON // Seams can rub, shorts can ride up, shirts can feel too baggy or too tight. When you find what you want to wear on race day, be sure to try it on and see how it fits and feels.

A recent trend in running apparel is compression-based socks and tights. There are a couple of theories regarding this technology. First, some contend that compression apparel can improve race day performance by increasing venous return and thus by-product (lactate) clearance. In theory, this would improve performance because you are able to run at a harder pace while still ridding your body of the stuff that causes you to slow down. Proponents of compression also point to its potential role in reducing delayed onset muscle soreness (DOMS) and thereby decreasing recovery time after hard training and racing. On the flip side, a recent article concluded that compression feels good but doesn't help the veins in the lower leg do their job any better. In fact, it was argued that post-run compression can lead to deep vein thrombosis (DVT) or a blood clot.

Because this type of apparel and the accompanying research are so new, the jury is still out on its effectiveness. Whatever you choose to wear on race day, make sure you have taken it for a few test runs first. Ideally, wear the outfit on a longer run so you know that with time and increased sweat output, the materials won't cause you any problems. After all the hard training you've put in, you really don't want to have a wardrobe malfunction on the big day.

Race
tactics

THE LAST THING YOU want is for your race to be undermined before you even get to the starting line. Race day nerves are common, but you have worked too hard to be dismantled by poor planning. There is no strategy on earth that can eliminate all the jitters and unknowns that might crop up, but certain steps can put you ahead of those who are not prepared. Focus on controlling the variables that you can and planning for the ones you can't. From your pre-race meal, to where you'll meet your family at the finish, to what shoes you're going to wear, to checking the weather and having the appropriate layers, planning ahead will go a long way toward keeping you calm when it matters. Going into race weekend, Plan A, along with Plan B and Plan C, should be well rehearsed and ready to be put into motion. When you're relaxed at the start line, you're less likely to make silly mistakes in the early stages of the race, keeping you focused and ready to follow protocol. We often caution runners not to underestimate the amount of planning a half-marathon requires. Consider the following factors as you make arrangements prior to race morning, remembering that your race will only be as good as your pre-race preparation, whether that is the training itself or getting to the start line on time.

Pre-race preparation

TRAVEL

If you are headed to a destination race, you'll probably have to arrange your travel plans months ahead of time. Besides needing to decide how to get to the race, you have to secure a place to stay. For the most part, cities that put on races with 35,000 or more runners will sell out of decent hotel rooms soon after race registration closes. Indeed, hotel rooms sometimes sell out as fast as the race entries. No doubt, you'll want a reasonably comfortable bed both before and after the race.

Many runners, especially first-timers, choose to sign up for a local race to avoid the extra costs and hassle associated with traveling. Even if your race is local, you still may want to consider getting a room. While sleeping in familiar surroundings is attractive to some, others would rather stay at a nearby hotel the night before so they can easily walk to the start line the next morning. There are a couple of advantages to this strategy. You are able to get a bit more shut-eye before rising for the big day. Too, if you are someone who gets stressed by the influx of crowds and chaos surrounding race morning, you might find walking just those few blocks to the start line eases your anxiety. If you prefer to sleep in your own bed the night before, be sure to leave early enough to get to the start. Although you may live only 15 minutes from where the race begins, traffic and parking can be a nightmare in any city on race day morning. Consider having someone drop you off so you don't have to figure out where to park.

STRATEGIC SPECTATING

Most runners welcome a friendly, familiar face along the course. It not only breaks up the monotony but also gives you something to look forward to as you grind through 13.1 miles. Despite this, don't spend time worrying about where and when you'll meet your family or friends. The best strategy here is to put someone else in charge. For the 2012 Olympic Trials marathon, I reserved hotel rooms and purchased plane tickets for my parents, but beyond that, my wife took care of the details. She set up itineraries, flew down to Houston with my parents, and made sure they got to their hotel. Beforehand she helped figure out where to find me along the course and the spot where we would meet at the finish. She knew that I needed to focus on my race during the days leading up to marathon weekend, so she picked up the slack and allowed me to forgo dealing with certain arrangements that were likely to stress me out. Consider this point person your captain and allow him or her to take control of details you would rather not handle.

In terms of where to direct your personal cheering squad along the course, it depends on what support you think you will need, and when. For some, the race is over in an hour or hour and a half, so it makes sense for your cheering quad to pick a spot that's close enough to the start to allow them to also get to the end and watch you finish. Alternately, you may want to have that support at a point where things may feel pretty grueling—maybe at around 10 miles. If you are in that latter group, seeing a friendly face, hearing words of encouragement, or being handed a special snack may be just the ticket at that late point in the race to get you through to the finish line. In this case, consider splitting up your cheering squad so that you also have someone waiting to watch you cross the finish line.

STUDY THE COURSE

Knowing the race course is a big advantage. If your race is local, consider getting out and running sections of the route periodically so you know what to expect come race day. If you know the turns, hills, and various other details of a course, a sense of familiarity is established. With familiarity come calm and control. The athletes in the Hansons-Brooks Distance Project will often take a trip to where we will be racing to run the course a few times. Doing this early in the training segment allows us to alter what and where we do our training to be fully prepared for the course. If you don't have the luxury of running the course prior to competition, check the official race website, YouTube, and the blogosphere for course tours and reviews.

Race weekend

THE RACE EXPO

Most race expos are akin to bustling flea markets. I'll admit that I sometimes love wandering the aisles, browsing the latest running shoes, gear, and goodies. Despite this, I urge you to avoid spending any length of time on your feet at the expo, a common mistake I see many runners make. They are in awe of the pageantry surrounding the big event, so they stand around on hard concrete floors in the convention hall instead of resting on their couch or hotel bed. For most Sunday races, the expo is open Friday and Saturday. If this is the case and you are able, go during your lunch hour on Friday and pick up your packet. This keeps you from lingering too long, so you can have a relaxed pre-race day. If you can't make it to the expo until the day before the race, go as early as possible to avoid the crowds and then get the heck out of there so you can go somewhere and put your feet up.

PRE-RACE DINNER

Whether you're attending an organized pre-race pasta dinner or staying home with your family to eat, the guidelines are the same. Most important, carbo-loading doesn't mean having four plates of spaghetti and three loaves of bread. Eat a regular-sized meal, but make sure it's healthy and high in easily digestible carbohydrates. The main goal is to top off those glycogen stores prior to the race. This is actually a goal for the last few days leading up to the race, so don't treat your pre-race dinner as your main source of carbo-loading. Indeed, this meal should cap off a balanced week of eating as suggested in the nutrition chapter; otherwise your pre-race dinner won't make much difference. Practice ahead of time by eating the same meals before your long runs so you know what to expect on race day. Additionally, while hydration is an ongoing process, make sure you use the day before the race to continue taking in water and sports drinks. Proper hydration takes time and should be tended to throughout the week.

BEFORE BED

Use the evening prior to the race to make sure all your t's are crossed and i's dotted. Your drop bag should be packed and ready to go, the timing chip fastened to your shoe, your clothes laid out, and your water bottle full. When you head to bed, chances are that sleep will be fairly hard to come by. Don't fret if you are tossing and turning. You should have banked plenty of rest over the past 10 days. If you do find yourself awake, consider grabbing a midnight snack, like an energy bar or a piece of fruit. While this isn't necessary, the body burns through about half of the glycogen stored in the liver during the overnight hours. By eating a late night snack, you further reduce how much you need to replace in the morning, potentially avoiding stomach upset. If you get especially nervous right before a race, this is a good way to consume calories before the jitters set in. Instead of needing 300–500 calories in the morning, you may be able to reduce that to just 100–200 calories to top off glycogen stores.

RACE MORNING

What you eat for your race morning meal depends on when you wake up. It's not uncommon for a runner to have trouble sleeping the night before a big race, so getting up early is often better than staying in bed and overanalyzing your race plan. The amount of time needed for digestion depends on the person; some runners need 3 full hours to digest a meal before running, but others only need 1. If you wake up 3 hours or more before the race, you can get away with chowing down on a normal breakfast, like a bagel with peanut butter, a banana, and coffee or juice. Any closer to gun time, however, and you need to be more conservative. As discussed earlier, within a few hours of the start, eat less solid food and mostly carbohydrates. With an hour to go, stick with something like an energy gel, which will satiate you for a short time but won't give you a full feeling. Furthermore, begin measuring your liquid intake by sips, not ounces. The last thing you want is to have water sloshing around in your stomach during the first half of the race. Eliminate wild card scenarios by planning everything from where you'll stand in the start corral to which port-a-john station you'll utilize. Hold on to your water bottle in the corral and continue sipping as you wait for fun time.

In addition to what you're putting in your body, you must consider what you're putting on it. Check the weather forecast for both before and during the race. If you end up standing in the corrals for 30 minutes or more, you'll want to be prepared. Weather in a spring or fall race can be unpredictable—often unseasonably warm or unseasonably cold. At the Detroit Marathon and Half-Marathon, for example, which is held in October, the weather can vary from 80-degree heat to near-blizzard conditions whipping across the Detroit River. Most years, the temperatures hover between 30 and 40 degrees, making wardrobe choices particularly tricky during the early morning hours. While your legs may go numb standing around before the sun fully rises, you'll feel fine once you begin running. This means that you'll need to wear layers to stay warm prior to the start, but then be able to easily shed garments as you warm up during the race.

One of the most common questions among runners in our training programs is whether they should wear nice running gear that they'll have to carry with them or something old they don't mind tossing to the curb. The Hansons solution is simple: Wear something you're willing to lose. For your bottom layer, sport your regular running gear with the race number attached, but over that, wear an old pair of sweatpants from the bottom of your dresser or a sweatshirt you wore to paint the living room. When you begin to warm up, which you will, you can throw off the top layer without a second thought. Just make sure to pin your number on the layer that you don't plan to take off during your race.

MENTAL PREPARATION

In my experience, the best way to mentally prepare yourself prior to a race is simply to be calm. Getting your heart rate up before you even start running is never a good idea. A good way to find that calm is to approach the race with "cautious confidence." Step back and spend a moment thinking about your training, reminding yourself that you are fit and ready to race. Training doesn't lie. Be realistic in pondering the difficulty of the race, but also remind yourself that all your training has prepared you to handle it.

Why does this approach work? For one, it forces you to slow down and accept that the task at hand is going to be hard and at times is going to hurt. This keeps you cautious to the point of avoiding over-zealous pacing right out of the gate. In addition, when the going gets tough during the race, you are prepared for it. You knew it wasn't going to be a cakewalk. By preparing this way, you are able to have positive and motivating thoughts ready and waiting to help you endure.

Race protocol

RACE TIME

Race time is go time. Once the starting gun goes off, it's time to cash in all those hard-earned chips. The most common question we get about race strategy regards mile splits. We have already discussed the physiological reasons behind pulling back on the reins and running a conservative pace the first half of the race, but there is more to it than that. Throughout training, many of your workouts are focused on running particular paces. We strongly believe in the truth attached to the old adage "Race the way you train," and we have emphasized even pacing during workouts in hopes of getting the same result on race day. More specifically, the training is meant to prepare you to run fairly predictable splits throughout, with the second half of the race slightly faster than the first, called a negative split strategy. We remind runners that going out slow will almost never cause any lasting damage to your overall pace, but starting too fast might. If you go out way ahead of pace and begin to fade, not only will your body feel the strain, but your mind also takes a beating as you get passed by other runners who started slower.

negative split strategy: This is a method of running the second half of a race faster than the first half.

> **even split strategy:** This is a method of running the first and second halves of a race in identical times.

What's more, every current world record from the 5K to the marathon has been set via negative or even splits. Most PRs are set that way too. When you start out at a pace you can maintain and then find yourself passing other runners who overestimated their abilities, you'll discover a newfound confidence in the later stages of the race. While many runners say that they feel the best at the beginning of the race and want to capitalize on that by banking time early on, this approach nearly always ends in disaster. A half-marathon is a substantial number of miles, and what feels like a comfortable pace at mile 2 may not feel so great at mile 10.

While you should remain steadfast in your race plan in most circumstances, flexibility may be required. Sometimes a fast result at the end of the day depends on getting lucky with a few variables, in particular, weather. It can be disappointing to train your hardest only to be met by 80-degree heat, hurricane winds, or even a monsoon. I know. I've been there and have the less-than-satisfying race times to prove it. In these situations, which will surely affect your race performance, it is easy to feel that all is lost. While there are plenty of quantifiable gains from training for a half-marathon, even if the stars don't align for a great race day, not being able to run your best performance can be heartbreaking. But weather is not something you can control, and you have to make the best of the situation. I remember facing challenging conditions during my senior year of college at the NCAA Cross Country Championships. It was so frigid that day that we actually had a team meeting to discuss the possibility of frostbite in an area you would least want to have frostbite. I remember the announcer giving us the 2-minute warning before the start and then saying, "It's a balmy 9 degrees, and with the wind chill, it's negative 13!" These were not ideal conditions, to be sure, and I was disappointed that the weather was not in my favor, but I wasn't going to let it stop me from putting forth my best effort. If your race day presents challenging conditions, remind yourself that everyone else is facing them, too. Take some time and consider the real reasons you decided to train for a half-marathon in the first place and the numerous benefits and personal growth that have resulted from training. Surely it is not a total loss, even if you have to adjust for a slower pace.

In the same way that we have emphasized smart training, you also must be wise about your race strategy. If the forecast has thrown a wrench in your original plans, alter the course of action accordingly to ensure you reach the finish line in one piece. From a temperature standpoint, you can expect to slow down anywhere from 5 to 8 seconds per mile when the temperatures reach the 60s and higher. Generally speaking, you would likely run 5 seconds slower per mile at 60 degrees, 10 seconds slower at 70 degrees, and 15 seconds slower at 80 degrees. This, of course, can depend on a number of factors. For instance, if you have been training in the heat for months, it's not going to affect you as much as it does other runners. The same goes for smaller runners as well as highly trained harriers. When it comes down to it, weather-related adjustments of expected finishing times vary depending on the individual.

RACE FUEL

For many runners of the half, the race day mantra to remember is simply this: Fuel and hydrate early and often. That said, you may be able to get away with less of both, depending on your speed. Unlike in the marathon, where a race can be made or broken on appropriate fueling, fueling for the half could have either a huge impact on the outcome or very little. A lot depends on how quickly you will complete 13.1 miles. If you are going to be on the course for less than 90 minutes, then fueling and hydration are a lesser concern during the race. At this pace, you will be finished with the race before your glycogen stores are depleted; you just need to make sure they are full at the start. If they are, you can be confident that you can finish strong without crashing into that brick wall that sometimes jumps out unexpectedly at runners on the course.

On the other hand, if you are running for 2 or more hours and fail to fuel properly along the course, you may find yourself feeling seriously drained well before the finish line. You will need to carefully consider your fueling plan, and the importance of starting calorie and fluid replacement early in the race cannot be stressed enough. Consider this: For elite runners, bottles of fluid containing each runner's own concoctions are generally placed every 5 kilometers. Physiologists tell us that the stomach can handle about 8 ounces of fluid every 15 minutes or so, which is about how long it takes elite men to run 5 kilometers. For the other 99.9 percent of runners who don't arrange access to their own bottles, there are water stops every 2 miles or so in most half-marathons. This means that if you take a cup of water or sports drink at every water stop, you'll be taking in fluids at about the same rate as the elites. The cups that are offered are usually 6–8 ounces, and they are generally filled with about 4–6 ounces of fluid. When you take into account average spillage, a runner can get 2–3 ounces at each station. Whether or not you stop or just grab a cup on the go is up to you. But remember, getting in the fluid and calories is of the utmost importance. A couple of seconds spent stopping to refuel or hydrate can actually save minutes in the long run by helping to prevent bonking. At each station, we suggest getting a cup at one of the first tables and then perhaps a second cup at the last table. In my experience, the calories offered in sports drinks are as important as the fluid itself. When runners "hit the wall," it's because they are out of sugar, and the sugar in sports drinks can help combat this occurrence. The only time this isn't an appropriate choice is if you have just taken a sports gel (or equivalent), which should be washed down with water. This will put you right in line with what most elites consume during an average half-marathon. While the sports drink is the best option in most cases, get your hands on whatever you can.

MIDRACE PACE ADJUSTMENTS

Over the years we've witnessed many runners who have gotten either significantly ahead or behind their desired paces early in the race. This is often a side effect of the crowded streets at the beginning of the race. Sometimes a runner will dash out at a clipped pace, in the hope of getting ahead of the crowd. In other cases, a runner is held back by the crowd for a few miles, and once out of the throng, he or she speeds up in hopes of getting back on track, making for extremely inconsistent mile splits. For instance, a half-marathoner with a 9:00-minute per mile goal pace may be slowed by the mob of runners leading the pack, causing him to run closer to 9:20 pace for the first several miles. As the crowds thin out around the 10K mark, he may feel he needs to make up for lost time, increasing his speed to 8:45 pace instead of getting back to the original plan of running 9:00-minute miles. As you have probably guessed from what we've said about pacing, this is a dangerous way to try to gain time. Instead, get settled back into your planned race pace and gradually pick it up over the next several miles to conserve energy and set yourself up for a strong second half.

Although you may feel great the first half of the race, that doesn't give you the green light to pick up the pace. I can't tell you how many runners I have seen cross the halfway point far ahead of schedule, only to crash and burn in the later miles. If adrenaline gets the best of you in the early stages of the race, prompting your pace to be faster than planned, don't panic. Just fix it. Slow down to goal pace and find the rhythm that will carry you for miles on end. Focus on your own race and try not to get caught up in what other runners are doing. If someone breezes past you, assume you'll catch him or her later on. In many cases, that's exactly what will happen.

Race day checklist

- ☐ shoes and socks
- ☐ singlet and/or sports bra
- ☐ shorts
- ☐ water/sports drink
- ☐ race number
- ☐ timing chip
- ☐ pins or race number belt
- ☐ energy gels
- ☐ watch
- ☐ sunglasses
- ☐ hat
- ☐ lip balm and/or sunscreen
- ☐ post-race clothes

- ☐ towel
- ☐ toilet paper or tissues
- ☐ antichafing lubricant (Bodyglide™ or petroleum jelly)
- ☐ Band-aids to protect nipples (for the guys)
- ☐ gloves/arm warmers
- ☐ throwaway shirt and/or pants
- ☐ money
- ☐ equipment check bag
- ☐ directions to start and pre-race instructions

When you head to the start line, we recommend consolidating everything you might need that you're not wearing into a clear bag, which is usually provided to you by the race. After the Boston Marathon tragedy, seemingly more and more races are providing these and making mandatory gear checks a security measure. Take everything with you to your waiting area, and then take only what you need to the starting corral. Leave the rest at the bag check station.

Post-race recovery

TRAINING USING THE HANSONS Method ends with your half-marathon, the culmination of 18 weeks of hard work. What happens after the race depends on the individual runner and his or her level of running. For example, a high-mileage veteran competitor may run a couple of half-marathons in a single training block. In contrast, a newbie may be completely wiped out and not ready to do another event in the near future. For the purpose of this chapter, let's discuss post-race recovery in terms of your half-marathon being the culmination of training and the end point of a training segment.

Taking time off from running after the race is important because it gives your body time to restore glycogen and hydration levels to normal. In addition to being depleted of all fuel sources, your exercising muscles feel the burn. How much and what kind of pain you feel the day after your race can vary; however, it's common to feel stiff, sore, and supremely worn-out. The half-marathon breaks down your muscles on a microscopic level, leaving them in need of rest and repair.

Consider the following your plan of action as soon as you cross that finish line.

Immediately after the race

It often happens that a runner reaches the finish line and then wonders, "Okay, now what?" We spend so much time focusing on training and racing, it is easy to forget to think about what comes after you reach the finish line. No matter what the clock says, as long as you gave the race your best shot, that's all that matters now. Take those first moments after the race to revel in the fact that you took your body to the edge and made it to the finish. Allow yourself a moment to be proud of this major accomplishment. Along with those positive feelings will most certainly come soreness and exhaustion. You may even think you will never do a race again. But while it can hurt, it's also true that after that first race, many runners are hooked.

First 30 minutes

The same general rules you follow after a workout also apply after your half-marathon. Regardless of your finish time, immediate action toward your recovery is crucial and will have a significant impact on when you can return to running. Although you may wince at the thought of eating, you need to try to consume some calories right away. The good news is that you can pretty much eat anything you are craving. It is the calories that are important, not their source. This is a good thing because you usually can't be picky when it comes to finish line fare. Whatever they are offering, take it. Because you have depleted much of your available muscle and liver glycogen, your body will bounce back far sooner if you do. What's more, your blood glucose is low, or on the verge of being so, you're dehydrated, and you have few remaining electrolytes. The faster you start replacing these nutrients, the sooner you'll be feeling back to normal. That window of optimal recovery time is small, so take advantage of the goodies in the finish chute that first 30 minutes after the race.

The first 2 hours

Once you have gathered your hardware and snacks, you can leave the finish chute and find your family and friends. As long as you have had something to eat and drink, you don't need to worry about consuming a full meal until your stomach settles down. If it isn't a hometown race, go back to your hotel, get cleaned up, and put on some comfortable clothes (and comfortable shoes, such as flip-flops or sandals). By that point you may be ready to sit down for lunch. Although you are probably tired of pasta, focus on taking in a high percentage of carbohydrates to replace all that lost glycogen. If you still aren't ready for a feast, steadily consume calories to get in a good amount over time. At this point, try to choose more nutritious foods to get your system back on track. Fruits, vegetables, and whole grains are all great options, along with water, fruit juice, or sports drinks. Again, the details you take care of now will help you down the line.

The rest of the day

Continue to hydrate and replace calories as desired. Put your feet up and relax for a few hours; you've earned it! Regardless of ability and how hard you pushed yourself during the race, you will likely notice at least some soreness over the rest of the day and into the following morning. Those first steps out of bed the day after the race may be labored, and walking up and down stairs may be an unpleasant challenge. From elites to weekend warriors, no one escapes a hard race without a little soreness.

Besides the glycogen depletion, the structural integrity of the muscles has been compromised, so don't plan any big outings right after your race. In my experience, your first half-marathon dishes out the most difficult recovery. The more you run over time, the easier the recovery seems.

The next 5–7 days

Don't run at all during this time. Some of you may be thinking that you don't need time off, but remember that we are approaching this from a long-term development standpoint. With long-term development, we take planned rest time now, and we can avoid unplanned rest time later on! We have learned that taking a break from running is generally very beneficial. Not only should you not run, but you also should avoid putting any new races on the calendar. Some runners fall into a cycle of jumping back into mileage just a few days after a big race, often leaving their legs feeling stale a month down the line. Instead, take the time off now, recover completely, and then go back to running. Enjoy the break and use this occasion to catch up on the things that took a backseat during training. Instead of worrying about your next workout or fitting in a long run, you can sleep in, read the newspaper, and regain some balance in your life. If exercise is a must, limit it to light aerobic activity such as cycling, using an elliptical, or something else that's not completely weight bearing.

TABLE **11.1** SAMPLE WEEK OF RETURN TO RUNNING: BEGINNER

MON	TUES	WED	THURS
20–30 min. of slow running	OFF or crosstraining/resistance training	OFF (same as Tuesday)	30 min. of slow running

After 1 week

Following your week's vacation, it's time to start running again. For first-time half-marathon finishers, we don't like to specify a time line for your return, other than to advise you to be cautious. Most veterans are itching to get running again after a week of rest. Although we love seeing this enthusiasm, one of the problems we often encounter is runners who want to begin planning their next race before they are even through the finish line chute. It is good to have goals, and we are always glad that a runner wants to continue training, but make sure you keep these plans flexible. For newbies and veterans alike, it is important to wait and see how recovery goes in order to avoid rushing back to running too soon.

Once you have established that you're fully recovered and ready to get back into your routine, we advise starting with an easy running regimen. Upon your return, you may be stiff, and those first few runs may be more difficult than usual. Don't worry; you haven't lost as much ground as you think. A week off will have decreased your fitness minimally. I am not saying you'll feel amazing on your first run back, but trust me, your fitness is still there. For new runners, try starting with 3–5 miles (about 30 minutes) every other day or so. The first week might look like the schedule in Table 11.1.

Veteran runners can be more aggressive in their return, but their effort should still be based on how the body reacts to resumed training.

FRI	SAT	SUN
OFF (same as Tuesday)	30 min. of slow running	OFF

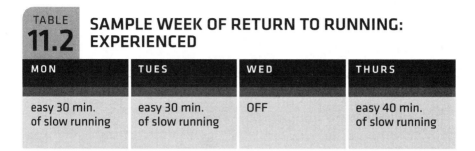

TABLE 11.2	SAMPLE WEEK OF RETURN TO RUNNING: EXPERIENCED		
MON	**TUES**	**WED**	**THURS**
easy 30 min. of slow running	easy 30 min. of slow running	OFF	easy 40 min. of slow running

An experienced runner's body is probably more accustomed to endurance training, making the comeback somewhat easier. Even so, every runner is different, and you should pay attention to what your body is telling you after your race. If something doesn't feel right or you are struggling to regain your form, we recommend backing off and letting the body heal itself. When you are ready to start some easy running again, a sample week for a veteran runner might look like the schedule in Table 11.2.

For all runners, resistance training can be picked up two or three times each week. This should be done on days that you won't be doing SOS workouts in the upcoming weeks, allowing you to get into a routine. For example, if you know that in the future you'll be doing SOS workouts on Tuesday, Thursday, and Sunday, establish your resistance training days on Monday, Wednesday, and/or Friday. By starting the regimen at this time, you can build running-specific strength without doing a single workout for several weeks.

After following the aforementioned mileage for the first week back in training, you might consider bringing things up a notch for the second week, although your running should still be all easy mileage. This is dependent on how your body responded to that first week. If you are feeling refreshed and looking forward to getting back on track, add a bit of mileage. The beginner should add 2 days with 30-minute runs,

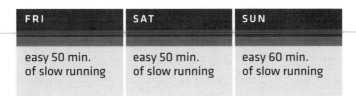

FRI	SAT	SUN
easy 50 min. of slow running	easy 50 min. of slow running	easy 60 min. of slow running

bringing the weekly total to 5 days of 30-minute runs each. Advanced runners can add time to each of their running days, aiming for 45–60 minutes of easy running, 6 days a week. If you are still feeling sore and tired, however, give yourself another week to linger at the lower mileage and let your body and mind recover.

Four to 6 weeks after the half-marathon

After those first 2 weeks of easy running, you should spend the next 2 weeks building mileage, allowing for a slow return to typical training volume. The Advanced Program peaks at about 50 miles, but the average mileage is around 40 miles per week, and the Beginner Program averages slightly less at 30–35 miles per week. The Just Finish Program is in the 20–25 miles per week range. Once you are comfortably running "average" weekly mileage again, you can begin structured training and start to draw up plans for new goal races. Whatever you choose to do, a training segment doesn't always need to adhere to an 18-week time frame. You may find that as you become more experienced, the length of time you need to prepare for a half-marathon can be shortened by a few weeks. In most cases, a speed or base-building segment can be 10–14 weeks. The more weekly mileage a person is able to tolerate, the shorter those training segments often need to be.

The great beyond

The question at this point is where to go from here. Many runners feel they need to get right back into half-marathon training, others may go back to shorter distances races, and still others will take the leap into marathon training. If you choose the last option, consider using a program from *Hansons Marathon Method*. The training plans are based on the same building blocks as our half-marathon plans, which will ease your transition to this new distance.

The downtime following your race offers an excellent opportunity to sit back and consider the timing of your long-term goals. For runners who just completed the Beginner Program or Just Finish Program, this can be an ideal time to build up mileage and perhaps gradually enter a more ambitious training regimen for a spring half-marathon. If that first race went well, this time gives you the chance to safely and slowly put mileage on your legs, preparing you for the increased training. The opportunities vary from runner to runner and can change as the seasons allow or geography permits.

Some runners decide to capitalize on the fitness base they have just built by dedicating a training segment to shorter races. As far as 5Ks and 10Ks, this is a great way to build speed and keep your legs feeling fresh rather than simply going right back into training for longer races. A 10-week speed section is especially well timed for runners who have just finished a half-marathon but want to return to the shorter races. These runners are strong from the half-marathon training, and a little shot of speed will make them faster overall.

Finally, half-marathoners may use the race and the accompanying training as a catalyst to build their mileage further and continue increasing their workouts in order to tackle the marathon distance. That can work well for the runner who did a spring or early summer half-marathon and wants to make the turnaround to do a fall marathon.

The same is true for a late fall or early winter half-marathon; a runner who has completed this distance can take on a spring marathon without worry. Whatever your choice, the experience you gain from the half-marathon distance will be helpful in any other running or racing you decide to do.

Appendix A

The Elite Program: Hansons-Brooks Distance Project

When Kevin and Keith Hanson took their experience and expertise to the elite running world in 1999, there was a significant shift at hand within the sport, with several competitive training groups springing up across the country with a shared mission of supporting American post-collegiate runners. Over the years, the African nations had begun to dominate distance running, leaving other countries, such as the United States, to step back and reevaluate how they trained their Olympic hopefuls. Accomplished and successful coaches, the Hansons knew they had the necessary tools and training methods to assist elite runners in their pursuit of international success. Thus the Hansons-Brooks Distance Project came to fruition.

Performances in the half-marathon of current and former Hansons-Brooks runners rival those of any elite program in the country. In the years since first forming, the squad has had 12 top 10 finishes in the USA Half Marathon Championships, including one champion with Brian Sell. Even more impressive, the team can boast 11 members of the IAAF World Half Marathon Championship squads. And yet, when you consider the project's roster of athletes, they have something interesting in common: Only a few of them were truly great runners in college. The lesson here is that development and success take time. While the majority of the runners recruited by the Hansons-Brooks Distance Project were only average to good collegiate athletes, many have gone on to achieve great success under the same training principles on which our programs in this book are based.

For another perspective on the building blocks upon which your training will rest, you may find it interesting to explore the related elements that are important to the elite runners we train. This not only dispels myths about how high-level runners actually train but also reveals the similarities between your own training and that of Olympians and Olympic hopefuls.

Just as we stress long-term development in this book's three training plans, so too do we focus on the long term in our Elite Program. Setting our sights on success far down the road is our goal when runners join the team. Indeed, Kevin and Keith seek to develop a runner over months and years, not cultivate a one-hit wonder who is prone to overtraining and burnout. The key to a runner's development, regardless of level, is patience. Allowing the body time to adapt to its current level before jumping to the next level is crucial. Appropriate work coupled with patience will yield the desired outcome and best results.

Because the half-marathon is a unique event of strength and speed, many of our postcollegiate runners simply need time to adjust from college-style workouts and seasons and develop into road racers. Taking time to build mileage and strength while maintaining their "college legs" (most college programs focus on 5K and 10K speed, since that's what they compete at) means that it may be a few years before they really become lethal at the half distance. For many of our elites, the half will ultimately serve as a stepping-stone between their 5K and 10K days and the full marathon.

While the underlying principle of long-term development under-scores all our half-marathon training programs, there are some out-ward differences between the training programs in this book and the Elite Program. For starters, the lives of most readers vary greatly from the existence of elite athletes, and our training plans appropriately reflect those differences. Despite the distinctions, however, you may be surprised to discover that your training isn't as different from that of an elite runner as you may have thought.

Elite Program components

9-DAY TRAINING CYCLE

In the early days of the Hansons-Brooks Distance Project, the weekly training cycle was similar to the plans within these pages. Elites ran a track workout on Tuesday, a tempo-type workout on Thursday, and then a long run on Sunday. Along the way, we switched to a 9-day training cycle that looks something like this:

SUNDAY // long 16–20 miles

MONDAY // easy 10–12 (a.m.); easy 4 (p.m.)

TUESDAY // same as Monday

WEDNESDAY // tempo run 8–10 miles (or some variation)

THURSDAY // same as Monday

FRIDAY // same as Monday

SATURDAY // track 5 miles' worth of speed about 10K pace

SUNDAY // same as Monday

MONDAY // same as previous Monday

The training mileage for an Elite Program runner remains fairly steady all year. For example, when I train for a marathon, my weekly volume ranges from 110 to 140 miles per week; when I am preparing for shorter races, my volume is still 100–120 miles per week. Within this mileage, traditional long runs every week are not always necessary. Because the volume of the easy days is 10 to 12 miles, or 1:10–1:24 in terms of time, runners gain many of the same desired aerobic adaptations as they would from a regular long run. This high mileage makes the 9-day cycle particularly advantageous because it allows for adequate rest while still working all the systems that are important to half-marathon development.

WEEKLY VOLUME

In looking at the example of a 9-day training stint in the Elite Program, you may have noted that the mileage is significantly higher than in the training plans in this book. While the Advanced Program peaks at around 50 miles per week, male elites will reach 120 miles per week, and female elites will hit 100–110 miles per week. When it comes to the elite training, there are a number of factors built into the plan that make such high mileage tolerable and productive.

The first factor is time. We aren't referring to 24 hours in a day or 7 days in a week, but rather the years of previous training that have slowly allowed for an increased volume of mileage. While most runners entering the development program aren't running more than 100 miles per week, the majority of them are logging 80–100 miles. The increased mileage makes the 9-day cycle especially important because instead of asking a 22-year-old runner to jump into 120-mile weeks with three hard workouts per week, the frequency of SOS workouts is cut to every third day, giving that runner the chance to increase volume through easy days. Sometimes the extra mileage hurts a runner's performances initially, but over time, adaptations occur, leading to steady improvements.

The second factor concerns recovery. In addition to fitting in more mileage at easier paces, the 9-day cycle allows for steady recovery between SOS workouts. Even with these extra recovery days, cumulative fatigue plays an important role in the Elite Program, but it is also balanced with injury prevention. When the volume of an easy day reaches between 16 and 20 miles, that extra day between SOS workouts is necessary to provide added recovery. Although these days are classified as "easy" in the Elite Program, they are often run at approximately marathon pace. For example, during peak mileage of training, easy runs are typically completed at a pace of 6:00–6:30 per mile, and long runs at about 5:30–6:30 per mile. The majority of runs are 1:45 to 2:00 minutes per mile slower than goal race pace. The other factors that make this higher-volume program manageable are the inherent benefits that go along with being part of a structured training group, like the Hansons-Brooks Distance Project. While all the runners in the program have another job in some capacity (besides running), their schedules allow them to take naps throughout the week, in addition to getting 8–10 hours of sleep a night. Let's face it, if you had the opportunity to take a 2-hour nap a couple of times per week, you'd probably be able to handle more weekly mileage too. The high mileage is also made easier by having running shoes from Brooks, keeping us outfitted through the miles. Additionally, our athletes have the advantage of access to chiropractors, physical therapists, and other medical professionals who understand runners and the unique injuries and issues related to the sport.

SOS WORKOUTS

Along with a higher overall volume of mileage, the mileage contained within SOS workouts is higher. This means that the volume of SOS mileage is proportionate to the overall training plan, whether you're looking at the plans in this book or at the Elite Program. By breaking down each SOS workout, you'll see how similar the Elite Program is to the ones we recommend here.

THE LONG RUN // Runners in the Hansons-Brooks Distance Project complete 20-plus-mile long runs, even during a half-marathon training segment. This is because mileage is based on percentage of weekly volume and the time it actually takes to complete the long run. In a typical 120-mile week, a 20-miler represents about 16–17 percent of the weekly volume. For me, a 20-mile long run takes between 1:55 and 2:10, which falls well within the guidelines we have described. On the other hand, a 16-mile long run completed by someone running 70 miles per week will account for approximately 23 percent of the total weekly volume. Typically, that 16-mile long run will take around the same 2:00-hour duration, eliciting virtually identical metabolic and physiological adaptations, despite the difference in actual miles.

SPEED SESSIONS // In the Beginner and Advanced Programs, the speed sessions total 3 miles of fast running. Generally you'll be running around 30–50 miles per week when you do these workouts, which means that speed will account for roughly 7.5 percent of the weekly volume. Meanwhile, the absolute volume of a speed session in the Elite Program is typically around 6 miles. With a weekly volume of 120 miles, that represents 5 percent of the total weekly volume. Again, the principle is the same: Speed represents a small percentage of weekly training while we focus on developing aerobic capabilities through sub–lactate threshold work.

STRENGTH SESSIONS // Strength sessions are a vital part of half-marathon development, regardless of the level of training. In the Beginner and Advanced Programs, these sessions include 6 miles of hard running to be completed during 40- to 50-mile weeks, accounting for 10–13 percent of weekly volume. In the Elite Program, strength workouts are usually between 9 and 12 miles, which is 10–11 percent of total weekly volume within a 120-mile week. Once again, absolute volume is greater, but the percentage of SOS mileage completed during the training week is proportionate across programs.

TEMPO RUNS // At its peak, the 7-mile tempo run is about 15 percent of weekly volume in the Beginner and Advanced Programs. The Elite Program also includes 7-mile tempo runs, meaning that this work makes up 12 percent of the weekly volume. The percentage here is slightly lower as a result of the variations in the tempo runs that the elite runners complete, to be discussed later. For the half-marathon, this is where the elite program differs the most. The elite program focuses more on longer intervals at race pace with short recovery, but total volume may be higher than doing a traditional tempo run.

ELITE PROGRAM WORKOUTS

Some signature workouts in our elite marathon program have gained national attention, such as the Simulator (26K tempo run) and the infamous 2 × 6-mile workout. However, with the half-marathon program, what we ask runners following the Beginner Program and the Advanced Program to do doesn't look that different from what the elites do, except for total volume. A few workouts that are staples in the Hansons training arsenal are worth mentioning here. Whatever we are training for, you'll see these workouts somewhere along the way in the elite program!

LONG RUN VARIATIONS

THE STEADY-STATE EFFORT // This is one of my personal favorites because it involves a high level of concentration, reduces boredom associated with repetitive training, and also stimulates important aerobic adaptations. I use this with runners who are experienced but can't feasibly increase their mileage because of other obligations and constraints. Scheduled well into training, when a runner's fitness is established, this workout begins like any other long run. Gradually the intensity increases until the athlete is running about 30 seconds slower than goal marathon pace, or about 1 minute per mile slower than half-marathon pace. That speed is then held for 50–75 percent of the run. By forcing the body to run at a significant effort, nearing the tipping point between using mostly fat and drawing upon those highly coveted carbohydrates, the aerobic threshold is stimulated. Because the body wants to conserve carbohydrates, it begins to adapt to that pace and maximize its fat-burning capabilities. Pacing precision is important here because if runners go too hard, they hit the wall prematurely, but if they run too slow, they miss out on some of the desired effects. This workout is also a good mental exercise because it is a long, tough effort that requires an athlete to maintain focus for an extended period.

TEMPO RUN VARIATIONS

THE CUTDOWN // Between 10 and 12 miles in length, this workout starts at a pace of 6:00 minutes per mile for the elite men in the program, which is within our easy range, and decreases by 10-second increments to half-marathon pace. A typical cutdown workout looks like this: 6:00, 6:00, 5:50, 5:40, 5:30, 5:20, 5:10, 5:00, 4:50. From experience, I can tell you that this workout often feels easy at the beginning, but it becomes increasingly challenging with each passing mile.

4 AND GO! // This is an 8-mile tempo run during which we run the first half at marathon pace and the second half either at a designated faster pace, usually half-marathon pace, or simply as fast as we can go. The goal is to start comfortable and finish fast!

STRENGTH WORKOUT VARIATIONS

2 MILES, 8 × 800, 2 MILES // This is a combination workout, where we run 2 miles at half-marathon pace. After a ½-mile jog, we then engage in 8 × ½ mile at a 10K pace with a short recovery. Then we will finish the workouts with another 2 miles at half-marathon pace. The goal is to stay at or above that lactate threshold point for much of the workout while changing turnover in the legs a little bit. It's a great workout, since the half-marathon is a blend of speed and strength, and this really teaches a runner to deal with discomfort.

Sample training log for Elite Program

The following program (Table A.1) is a log of my training for October 2010 to February 2011, as I prepared for the Rock 'n' Roll Mardi Gras Half-Marathon. While this is tailored to my individual needs, it is a typical half-marathon training program for a veteran runner who is part of the Hansons-Brooks Distance Project. The only real difference in what our elite women runners do relates to pace, as they also run 100 or more miles per week during part of their half-marathon training. You'll notice that there are no big secrets when it comes to training an elite runner. In fact, the principles used are the same for everyone.

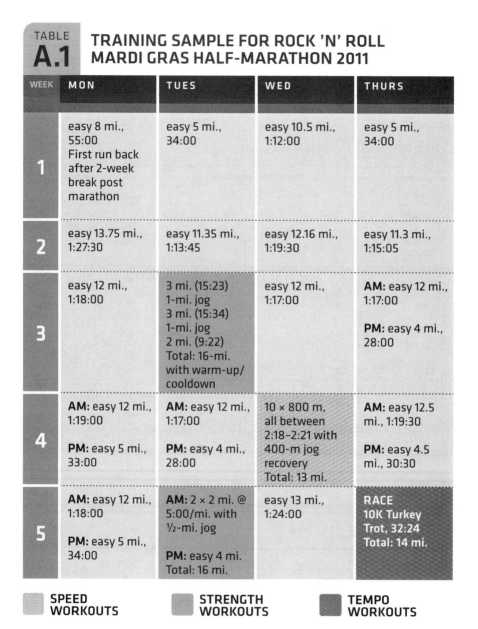

TABLE **A.1**	**TRAINING SAMPLE FOR ROCK 'N' ROLL MARDI GRAS HALF-MARATHON 2011**			
WEEK	MON	TUES	WED	THURS
1	easy 8 mi., 55:00 First run back after 2-week break post marathon	easy 5 mi., 34:00	easy 10.5 mi., 1:12:00	easy 5 mi., 34:00
2	easy 13.75 mi., 1:27:30	easy 11.35 mi., 1:13:45	easy 12.16 mi., 1:19:30	easy 11.3 mi., 1:15:05
3	easy 12 mi., 1:18:00	3 mi. (15:23) 1-mi. jog 3 mi. (15:34) 1-mi. jog 2 mi. (9:22) Total: 16-mi. with warm-up/ cooldown	easy 12 mi., 1:17:00	AM: easy 12 mi., 1:17:00 PM: easy 4 mi., 28:00
4	AM: easy 12 mi., 1:19:00 PM: easy 5 mi., 33:00	AM: easy 12 mi., 1:17:00 PM: easy 4 mi., 28:00	10 × 800 m, all between 2:18–2:21 with 400-m jog recovery Total: 13 mi.	AM: easy 12.5 mi., 1:19:30 PM: easy 4.5 mi., 30:30
5	AM: easy 12 mi., 1:18:00 PM: easy 5 mi., 34:00	AM: 2 × 2 mi. @ 5:00/mi. with ½-mi. jog PM: easy 4 mi. Total: 16 mi.	easy 13 mi., 1:24:00	RACE 10K Turkey Trot, 32:24 Total: 14 mi.

SPEED WORKOUTS   **STRENGTH WORKOUTS**   **TEMPO WORKOUTS**

FRI	SAT	SUN	WEEKLY TOTAL	WEEK
easy 12 mi., 1:20:00	easy 5 mi., 34:00	OFF	▶ **48.5** MI.	1
easy 11 mi., 1:11:36	easy 8 mi., 43:16	easy 12 mi., 1:14:39	▶ **79.56** MI.	2
5 × 1 mi., all between 4:43–4:48 with 600-m jog recovery Total: 13 mi.	**AM:** easy 12 mi., 1:16:00 **PM:** easy 4 mi., 28:00	long run, 16 mi., 1:40:00	▶ **101** MI.	3
AM: easy 12 mi., 1:20:00 **PM:** easy 5 mi., 33:00	4 × 1.5 mi. @ 4:50/mi. with 800-m jog recovery Total: 13 mi.	**AM:** easy 12 mi., 1:20:00 **PM:** easy 4 mi., 27:50	▶ **109** MI.	4
AM: easy 12 mi., 1:22:00 **PM:** easy 5 mi., 34:00	**AM:** easy 12 mi., 1:18:00 **PM:** easy 5 mi., 34:00	**AM:** easy 12 mi., 1:19:00 **PM:** easy 5 mi., 35:00	▶ **111** MI.	5

CONTINUES ↘

TABLE A.1 TRAINING SAMPLE FOR ROCK 'N' ROLL MARDI GRAS HALF-MARATHON, CONTINUED

WEEK	MON	TUES	WED	THURS
6	long run, 16 mi., 1:41:00	**AM:** easy 12 mi., 1:20:00 **PM:** easy 6 mi., 39:40	**AM:** easy 12 mi., 1:19:00 **PM:** easy 5 mi., 33:20	**AM:** 5 × 1 mi. @ 4:45/mi. with 800-m jog recovery **PM:** 4 mi., 28:00 Total: 19 mi.
7	**AM:** easy 12 mi., 1:20:00 **PM:** easy 5 mi., 33:30	**AM:** easy 13 mi., 1:29:20 **PM:** easy 4 mi., 28:00	2 × 3 mi. @ 5:10/mi. with 1-mi. jog Total: 13 mi.	**AM:** easy 10 mi., 1:08:00 **PM:** easy 4 mi., 28:00
8	**AM:** easy 12 mi., 1:25:00 **PM:** easy 5 mi., 34:00	**AM:** easy 12 mi., 1:24:00 **PM:** easy 6 mi., 40:00	2 × 4 mi. @ 5:10/mi. with 1-mi. jog recovery Total: 15 mi.	**AM:** easy 12 mi., 1:24:00 **PM:** easy 5 mi., 34:00
9	**AM:** easy 12 mi., 1:21:30 **PM:** easy 5 mi., 33:00	10 × 800 on roads @ 2:17/mi. with 400-m jog recovery Total: 16 mi.	**AM:** easy 12 mi., 1:22:00 **PM:** easy 5 mi., 34:00	**AM:** easy 12 mi., 1:23:00 **PM:** easy 4 mi., 28:00
10	easy 10 mi., 1:07:00	2 × 3 mi. @ 5:05/mi. with 1-mi. jog recovery Total: 13 mi.	**AM:** easy 13 mi., 1:29:00 **PM:** easy 4 mi., 28:00	**AM:** easy 10 mi., 1:08:00 **PM:** easy 5 mi., 34:00

SPEED WORKOUTS | STRENGTH WORKOUTS | TEMPO WORKOUTS

FRI	SAT	SUN	WEEKLY TOTAL	WEEK
easy 12 mi., 1:20:00	AM: easy 13 mi., 1:25:00 PM: easy 4 mi., 28:00	4 × 1.5 mi. Effort-based due to extreme hills and conditions Total: 17 mi.	▸ **116** MI.	6
easy 8 mi., 55:00	U.S. Club XC Championships 10K, 29:57, 10th place Total: 15 mi.	easy 10 mi.	▸ **94** MI.	7
AM: easy 12 mi., 1:23:00 PM: easy 4 mi., 27:15	4-3-2-1 (20:25, 19:55, 9:48, 4:35) Total: 19 mi.	easy 13 mi., 1:28:00	▸ **115** MI.	8
long run, 20 mi., 2:16:00	easy 14 mi., 1:38:00	easy 10 mi., 1:08:00	▸ **110** MI.	9
AM: easy 6 mi., 40:00 PM: RACE, 5K, 14:35 Total: 15 mi.	easy 16 mi., 1:45:00	AM: easy 11 mi., 1:15:00 PM: easy 5 mi., 34:00	▸ **108** MI.	10

CONTINUES ↘

TABLE A.1	TRAINING SAMPLE FOR ROCK 'N' ROLL MARDI GRAS HALF-MARATHON, CONTINUED			
WEEK	**MON**	**TUES**	**WED**	**THURS**
11	3 × 3 mi. @ 4:55/mi. with 1-mi. jog recovery Total: 17 mi.	AM: easy 13 mi., 1:29:00 PM: easy 5 mi., 34:00	easy 12 mi., 1:21:00	2 mi. @ 9:55 8 × 800 @ 2:20 with 400 jog 2 mi. @ 10:05 Total: 17 mi.
12	AM: easy 10 mi., 1:08:00 PM: easy 4 mi., 27:00	AM: easy 8 mi., 54:00 PM: easy 4 mi., 27:00	5 × 1 mi. @ 4:45 with 800-m jog recovery Total: 12 mi.	AM: easy 10 mi., 1:08:00 PM: easy 4 mi., 27:00
13	long run, 15 mi., 1:33:00	AM: easy 12 mi., 1:17:00 PM: easy 4 mi., 27:00	AM: easy 10 mi., 1:05:00 PM: easy 4 mi., 27:00	3 × 3 mi. @ 4:50/mi. Total: 17 mi.
14	AM: easy 12 mi., 1:22:00 PM: easy 5 mi., 34:00	AM: easy 10 mi., 1:08:00 PM: easy 5 mi., 34:00	3-2-1 @ 4:57/mi. with 1-mi. jog recovery Total: 14 mi.	AM: easy 12 mi., 1:22:00 PM: easy 5 mi., 34:00
15	AM: easy 10 mi., 1:10:00 PM: easy 5 mi., 34:00	AM: easy 12 mi., 1:17:00 PM: easy 5 mi., 34:00	long run, 18 mi., 1:51:00	easy 12 mi., 1:22:00
16	AM: easy 10 mi., 1:05:00 PM: easy 4 mi., 28:00	4 × 1.5 mi. @ 5:00/mi. with 800-m jog recovery Total: 14 mi.	AM: easy 8 mi., 55:00 PM: easy 4 mi., 28:00	easy 8 mi., 55:00

SPEED WORKOUTS   STRENGTH WORKOUTS   TEMPO WORKOUTS

FRI	SAT	SUN	WEEKLY TOTAL	WEEK
AM: easy 13 mi., 1:28:00 **PM:** easy 4 mi., 27:30	easy 12 mi., 1:19:00	8 mi. cutting down from 6:00–4:50/mi. Total: 14 mi.	▸ **107** MI.	11
AM: easy 4 mi., 28:00 **PM:** easy 4 mi., 28:00	**RACE** Half-marathon 1:05:43 in Naples, FL Total: 20 mi.	easy 10 mi., 1:09:00	▸ **90** MI.	12
AM: easy 11 mi., 1:17:00 **PM:** easy 5 mi., 34:00	**AM:** easy 10 mi., 1:08:00 **PM:** easy 5 mi., 34:00	6 × 1.5 mi. @ 5:00/mi. Total: 15.5 mi.	▸ **108.5** MI.	13
AM: easy 10 mi., 1:07:00 **PM:** easy 4 mi., 27:00	2 × 4 mi. @ 5:05/mi. with 1-mi. jog recovery Total: 15.5 mi.	easy 12 mi., 1:22:00	▸ **104** MI.	14
AM: easy 10 mi., 1:07:00 **PM:** easy 4 mi., 27:00	3-2-3-1 @ 4:57/mi. with 800-m jog recovery Total: 17 mi.	**AM:** easy 10 mi., 1:08:00 **PM:** easy 4 mi., 27:00	▸ **107** MI.	15
easy 6 mi., 40:00	**RACE** Half-marathon, 1:03:57 (4:54/mi.) 2nd place. NEW PR!	easy 4 mi., not timed!	▸ **78** MI.	16

Appendix B

TABLE A.2	SWEAT LOSS CALCULATOR

1	**CHECK WEIGHT* BEFORE AND AFTER TRAINING TO CALCULATE WEIGHT LOSS.** weight before ☐ weight after ☐ amount of weight lost ☐ oz. (ml) * Check weight without clothing, if possible. time period (1 hour preferable) ☐
2	**CONVERT AMOUNT OF WEIGHT LOSS TO OUNCES (MILLILITERS) OF FLUID.** e.g., a 2-lb. weight loss = 30 oz. of fluid / e.g., a l-kg weight loss = 1,000 ml of fluid ☐ oz. (ml) of fluid lost
3	**RECORD AMOUNT OF FLUID CONSUMED DURING TRAINING SESSION.** e.g., squeeze bottles are 20–24 oz./600–720 ml ☐ oz. (ml) of fluid consumed
4	**ADD AMOUNT OF FLUID LOST AND FLUID CONSUMED.** fluid lost + fluid consumed = ☐ oz. (ml)
5	**DIVIDE TOTAL OZ. (ML) OF WEIGHT LOSS BY NUMBER OF HOURS OF TRAINING TO DETERMINE AMOUNT OF OZ. LOST IN SWEAT PER HOUR.** total fluid lost ÷ hours of training = ☐ fluid losses in oz. (ml) per hour

EXAMPLE:

1–2. Weight before training: 165 lb. (75 kg); Weight after training: 164 lb. (74 kg)
Total weight loss: 1 lb. (0.5 kg) = 15 oz. (500 ml) fluid

3. Consumed 30 oz. (960 ml) fluid during 1-hour bike ride: 30 oz. (960 ml) fluid

4. Add fluid lost and fluid consumed: 15 oz. (500 ml) + 30 oz. (960 ml) = 45 oz. (1,460 ml)

5. Divide total sum of weight loss by hours of training: 45 oz. (1,060 ml) ÷ 1 hour of training = 45 oz. per hour for sweat losses

Index

Page references followed by f *denote figures. Page references followed by* t *denote tables.*

About the authors

Luke Humphrey began running track in middle school and hasn't slowed down since. After several all-state performances in high school, Luke ran for Central Michigan University from 1999 to 2004. There he was part of several NCAA Division I top-25 cross-country teams, including a 9th-place team finish in 2002. In 2004, Luke competed in his first marathon at the LaSalle Bank Chicago Marathon in the fall of 2004 for the Hansons-Brooks Distance Project. He

ran a debut time of 2:18:46 and was 18th overall. Since then Luke has gone on to finish 11th in the 2006 Boston Marathon, 11th in the 2008 ING New York City Marathon, and 12th in the 2010 Bank of America Chicago Marathon as well as to qualify for two U.S. Olympic Trials for the marathon (2008 and 2012). Luke holds a personal best of 2:14:38 in the marathon. He has a B.A.A. in exercise science from Central Michigan University and an M.S. in exercise science from Oakland University. Luke began Hansons Coaching Services in May 2006 to help runners of all abilities reach their running goals. He is the author of *Hansons Marathon Method.* He and his wife, Nicole, have a daughter, Josephine.

Keith and Kevin Hanson are cofounders of the Hansons-Brooks Distance Project, together coaching the Olympic development team to victories on national and international stages. They also co-own the Hansons Running Shops and avidly support, build, and encourage the running community, coaching hundreds of local runners to their first or 100th marathon.

ALSO AVAILABLE FROM VELOPRESS

HANSONS
MARATHON METHOD

A RENEGADE PATH TO YOUR FASTEST MARATHON

HANSONS
MARATHON
METHOD

LUKE HUMPHREY WITH KEITH & KEVIN HANSON

Paperback with illustrations and tables throughout
6" x 9", 256 pp., $18.95, 9781934030851

For the first time ever, you can train for your fastest marathon the Hansons way. The coaches of the Hansons-Brooks Distance Project have revealed the innovative system they use to train runners into race winners, national champions, and Olympians. From your first workout through your post-race recovery meal, you can train like a Hansons runner.

Available in bookstores, running shops, and online.
Learn more about VeloPress books for runners at velopress.com.

ALSO AVAILABLE FROM VELOPRESS

GET LEAN, GET FASTER

6" x 9", 296 pp., $18.95, 9781934030998
Paperback with tables and illustrations throughout.

The fastest athletes are the leanest. Lean athletes waste less energy, dissipate heat faster, and even gain more fitness from every workout. But for many reasons, dieting is dangerous for athletes. You need *Racing Weight*, the proven weight-management program for runners, cyclists, and triathletes.

The new edition of *Racing Weight* is based on the latest science—and the best practices of elite athletes. Six simple steps will get you to your fastest weight. You'll improve your diet, manage your appetite, balance your energy sources, time your meals and snacks, train for leanness, and monitor your weight and performance. **Get faster with *Racing Weight*.**

Available in bookstores, running shops, and online.
See more VeloPress books on weight loss and nutrition at velopress.com.